A story about fathers and sons. A story about professional sport, and what it takes to make the grade. A story about love, life, traveling and reflecting. And there is even a bit about restrooms.

Patrick Gilligan graduated with an honors degree in Equine Studies. After a decade as an exercise rider, he went on to spend 16 years training Thoroughbred racehorses in Newmarket in Suffolk, England. Now based in Lexington Kentucky, he is still active within the Thoroughbred industry.

Jack Gilligan rode his first winner at age 16 on only his second career mount at 33/1 at Newbury racecourse, in Berkshire England, on a horse trained by his father. Since moving to Kentucky in late 2014 Jack has ridden over 250 winners.

Around Kentucky
With the Bug!

Around Kentucky
With the Bug!

Patrick Lawrence Gilligan

ISBN Hardcover: 978-1-7328892-0-0
ISBN Paperback: 978-1-7328892-1-7
ISBN eBook: 978-1-7328892-2-4

Printed in the United States of America

Front Cover Photo: Courtesy of Coady Photography
Back Cover Photo: Courtesy of Kristina Taylor
Cover and Interior Design: Ghislain Viau

For Vicky & Jack

Contents

Introduction

I have flashes of memories of myself as a young child in America. The sort of unlinked fragments that, later in life, one might have after a heavy night on the town.

Snapshots of an event, impressions—the important things. My tractor, my Tonka crane, the ice cream truck. I remember the driver had the same name as me, Pat, and he had a money change machine on a belt around his waist. He had the best job in the world, Pat.

I was born on October 11, 1965, in Mount Vernon, just north of the Bronx, before we moved to a place called Haverstraw about thirty miles north of Manhattan. I remember how hot it was in the summer. A New York Summer. I remember crying at the heat.

I remember my father taking us to the circus, to the movies to see *Chitty Chitty Bang Bang*. I remember taking the

1

wheels off my tractor and replacing them with my mother's records. That didn't work out. For me or the records.

I remember finding a snake under my toy wheelbarrow. It was a copperhead; they are venomous. I kept lifting the upside-down barrow to peer at it until, eventually, I went in and told the babysitter. I think the neighbour got it.

And I remember winter. A New York Winter. The cold. The snow. I remember crying at the cold. Going sledding, falling off. Crying at that. I remember all the snow being ploughed into the centre of the courtyard where we lived. The bigger kids made tunnels through it.

I remember my father coming home with a nice green car, a Mercury. I remember my gold jacket. I liked that jacket. I stood out when we went to England. Not many five-year-olds were wearing gold in England back then. Wearing gold and wheezing, that's what I stood out for back then.

I remember the first day we were in England. I remember landing at Heathrow. We flew Pan Am, a big jet. It might have been one of the recently introduced Boeing 747s. I remember seeing London from the sky for the first time.

My uncle met us at Heathrow. I had convinced myself that he would have a beard, but he disappointed me. We went to my grandmother's council flat in Balham, South London. It was exciting. Everything was different. I discovered cereals without sugar. Soda without ice. Buses not cars. Walking not cars. Trains not cars. Never cars anymore—no one we knew seemed to own one.

The weather in London didn't make me cry, but it did make me wheeze. A lot. When the fog came, all I could do was wheeze. There isn't so much fog in England anymore; I don't miss it.

I had to leave a lot of stuff behind in America, my tractor, my Tonka crane, even my father. He didn't come. He didn't even know we were coming. You don't ponder that stuff when you are five. I think he must have though.

It was cosy, my grandmother's place. Besides her, there was my uncle, my mother, and me, plus my big sister, Eileen, and my little brother, Sean. And two bedrooms. I can't remember the sleeping arrangements, but we managed. My uncle stayed a lot with girlfriends. He was good like that.

I started school just around the corner. I hadn't been to school before. No one told me about that before we moved. No one told me that was part of the deal.

It was a big, ugly, austere place from the outside. It wasn't much better inside. But it got the job done, I learned to reed and rit. A lot of kids cry on their first day at school. I don't think I did. I don't remember crying much after we came to England.

Over the next few years we settled into English life. We moved out of my grandmother's place, and into a maisonette in Tooting, South London. Then a year or so later, we moved out to Worcester Park in Surrey. It was nice there, but it was during this time that my father passed away. People always said what a good driver he was, but he drove fast, and on this occasion the car left the road and plunged into a lake. We went back for the funeral. I didn't like that. I have tried to avoid funerals ever since. I don't even want to go to my own.

About a year after that we moved out to a nice home in Banstead, near Epsom in Surrey. That was quite a lot of moving by the age of eleven, and my mother had a curious habit of not telling me, or my younger brother, Sean, in advance. She told my older sister, but not us. So, my brother and I would regularly wake up to find all our stuff had been packed overnight. And we would be off. No goodbyes to our friends on the street. That's a bit odd really now, when I look back on it.

Banstead was a shock after New York and London. A neat tidy suburb, with immaculate gardens and mowed lawns. The road we lived on was the quietest thing we had encountered in our lives. In the early days, if we heard a car we would all rush to the window - even my mother with our new stepfather.

It was in Banstead that my mother and stepfather offered to take us for pony riding lessons. Maybe not the smartest move, looking back, considering I was a chronic asthmatic, allergic to horse hair, hay, straw, and dust in general.

But I loved it. It exhilarated me, and scared me a bit too, and it was tough to do, difficult to learn. I didn't find it easy, and for some reason that made me want to do it more.

I remember being sat on some geriatric pony in a riding arena, a bored teenager leading me around as I looked on in awe at the kids who could trot and canter unled. I suppose,

since in the end, my job was to break in and ride Thoroughbred racehorses, and gallop them flat out, and school them
over fences at speed, and even ride in some races, that I came
a long way.

Ponies became a big thing in my life, and I began to plot
how I would get my own. Every day I would ask if I could get
a pony. And every day I would be told no, that they couldn't
afford it.

I asked this nearly every day for two years, and when my
brother and sister flew back to the States to visit family for
a holiday, I said I would stay and save that money instead
for a pony. And every day at school I would sell my lunch to
the other kids, and save that money too. I don't know if my
mother wondered where the money came from, or why I had
lost so much weight, but she never said anything. You don't
pay as much attention when you have three children.

After two years my plan worked. We went and bought a
cheap pony from a horse dealer. He was ten years old, steel
grey, and one day I got home from school and there he was,
in our back garden. Which was a great surprise to me, and the
neighbours. And presumably to the pony as well.

I had assumed when I was begging for a pony that a saddle
would be part of the deal. That's the thing about assumptions.
The pony came with a bridle though, and that was enough
for me. Within a couple of weeks, I went from novice rider
to bareback daredevil careering around our garden, taking on
jumps built from garden chairs and brooms and bits of wood.

Like a Native American. Or a Traveller. The neighbours still looked surprised.

I just kept riding. It just carried on. And although I was bright enough, I was more smitten with horses. And even though I was an avid reader, I found school boring and would fake asthma attacks and just straight skip school, in order to ride. And since my stepfather liked to gamble on "the horses," and since we lived a stone's throw from Epsom racecourse, I became interested in the sport of horse racing. So, as soon as I had finished my exams, I was off. To go and become the greatest jockey the world had ever seen!

Going to work in a racing stable was a lot like going to prison back then. I headed off to a yard in Wantage in Oxfordshire, where I would live in the grooms' accommodation. There were cat droppings under the bed, girly magazines in the bathroom, and bunk beds. And when I opened the wardrobe door to put my clothes in, it came away from its hinges and hit me on the head.

You worked twelve and a half days out of every fourteen, and for the first two weeks, as I was "on trial," I was paid ten pounds. The environment was harsh, as blue collar as it gets, totally male. Tough enough. But I had gone to a rough-around-the-edges all-boys school, so I fitted in all right. The horses were something else though.

Thoroughbreds are not like other horses. They have been selectively bred for over three hundred years. An artificial breed. Three highly-strung, fine-boned Arabian stallions, imported to

England and bred to sturdy native English mares. It was like a romantic liaison between Rowan Atkinson and Rustie Lee somehow producing Usain Bolt. It shouldn't have worked, but somehow it did. The resultant offspring were swifter and more athletic than either of their parents. Hybrid vigour.

And from those beginnings, the breed was honed using one criteria only. Is it fast? The swiftest were bred to the swiftest, without a nod to temperament or any other quality.

And what they ended up with, three centuries later, was a half-ton of the fastest psychopaths on Earth. That's not fair really. Only some of them are psychopaths. Some are just neurotic, or bad tempered, or disobliging. And some of them are kind and noble and comforting.

I thought I could ride. I could jump my pony over a five-foot obstacle without thinking. But I had never ridden a Thoroughbred before. Never ridden a racehorse in training before. Horses trained and honed, and fed as athletes. Professional athletes. Faster, stronger, bigger, more aggressive. Professionals, used to being dealt with by professionals—not by green kids.

I couldn't manage them in the stable, and I certainly couldn't ride them in full exercise. I was reduced to riding the "sick, lame and lazy" around the country lanes of Wantage, just walking and trotting. Giving me time to reflect on my newly reduced opinion of my own abilities.

You see to go from riding a pony to piloting a fully fit Thoroughbred racehorse is like getting off a rusty bicycle and stepping into a Learjet. They are in perpetual go mode; they will take off given the slightest excuse. They are not like normal equines, not one bit. They are not toys, they can accelerate zero to forty miles an hour in a few seconds. They are physically stronger than half a dozen men. And they are fed and trained to make them as fast, aggressive and fit as they can be. It's a hell of a thing to ride a racehorse.

It took time. I was back to those days as a kid on the riding-school pony, looking at the bigger kids doing things I couldn't. But, in the end I got there, I became one of the lads, learned to handle Thoroughbreds, to ride them, to stay on when they bucked and reared and spun. To laugh at it, to enjoy it. To become good at it.

I moved back to work in Epsom, and for the next couple of years I averaged three hours a day riding. You become good at something you practice that much. I hardly took a day off the first two years I worked in racing. I rode every day, gaining experience, improving, and getting fit and strong. You don't see many out-of-condition people riding racehorses. It was hard work. And it worked the nerves out of me. The anxiousness I had carried with me most of my life dissipated, disappeared. I became carefree, got my first cheap car, loved it all.

Riding home early in the morning after a gallop, among your friends. Nature closer, away from the rat race. You could keep the normal world. No suit for me, no commute. Life was great. I suppose it was as close as an American could get to being a cowboy in Surrey.

I managed a couple of rides in races. But I wasn't enough of an athlete, my lungs weren't up to the job. So, I became an exercise rider, which was fun. But I had some ambition, so I went to night school and studied law and economics.

After my studies, I briefly tried a spell as a claims negotiator for a big insurance company, but it bored me, and I realized office life was never going to be my life. Later, I worked on building sites for a while, and as a bartender in London after I bought a property with my cousin and needed to earn more than racing jobs would pay. But always, eventually, I would drift back to the horses, to working in stables, a life I enjoyed, but one without much of a career ladder.

And that was about it. Until, one day a friend of mine noticed an article in the *Racing Post*. It was all about a new degree at Coventry University, the first of its kind in Europe. It was a degree in horses.

My old schoolfriend and I decided to apply. A chef with a gambling problem and a failed jockey. And we were accepted, mainly I think, because we were two of only about five males who did apply.

The next three years were fun. We were a bit older than most of the other students. And, having been working for the best part of a decade, at first we found them a little immature. But by the end, I was probably the biggest kid there. You could ask my wife, Vicky, because that is where we met.

I enjoyed learning about the horse, *Equus caballus*. And as I studied equine nutrition and anatomy and exercise physiology, I began to apply the theoretical knowledge I was gaining to my practical experience of working in racing stables and exercising horses. And I began to think about how I would train a racehorse myself.

After graduation, I was fired up and applied to dozens of trainers hoping for an assistant trainer position. All I got were rejection letters. Except one, from a trainer who called me for interview then conducted the whole thing with his back to me. Didn't turn around once, didn't greet me formally or otherwise, and dismissed me with a sniff. It turned out nobody wanted an assistant who could ride any racehorse and had a relevant degree.

Well, if you can't join them, beat them. So, I thought *Screw being an assistant.* And I went back to my stepfather and started asking him for a horse again...

I didn't get a horse. But I did manage, after a lot of begging, to get two thousand pounds. Not much to start a twenty-year career in racehorse training with. But I ignored all the naysayers, joined forces with another ex–equine studies student, and between us we bought two cheap unbroken yearlings from Tattersalls bloodstock auctioneers in Newmarket. The partner soon wanted out, but I managed to sell some shares in these prospective racers to family and friends—including the chef, and my brother and my sister and her future husband—and I was, just about, in business.

To cut a long story short, one cost a couple of thousand pounds and turned out to be useless. The other cost five hundred pounds, Vicky named him Rushcutter Bay. He went on to become a graded stakes winner, and, for a period, one of the best sprinters in Europe. And a career, of sorts, was born.

*What follows are my thoughts, reflections, musings,
writings and a historical account of my year around
Kentucky with my son, as he attempted to establish
himself as a jockey
in the USA. I hope you enjoy it.*

Chapter 1

America. Why? Why Not?

I'm not sure there was one thing that ultimately triggered our decision to finally make the oft-discussed move to the United States. It was, I suppose, in some part a result of my own half-baked ideological musings about America and its promise of opportunity. But in reality, it was mostly my son, Jack, who was the catalyst. It was his desire to pursue his career as a jockey stateside that turned me from couch-potato preacher into intercontinental adventurer.

Newmarket, in Suffolk, England, is the historic seat of Thoroughbred racing. A unique place that grew and prospered when the surrounding heathland found favour among the aristocracy, and indeed the monarchy, as a venue for matching their swiftest horses. King James I built a palace there back in

1610 and over the centuries magnificent private stables were established, until eventually, the town and the sport were utterly entwined.

By the time I arrived there in 1995, with a determination to become a racehorse trainer in my own right, the town was home to around sixty trainers—including many, if not most, of the biggest names in the sport.

I probably had no right to be there really, amongst the great and the good.

My career as a racehorse trainer started brightly though. Two stakes victories from my first 150 runners had people taking notice of someone who had shown up in town with a saddle, bridle, fifty pounds in his pocket, and two bargain basement yearlings.

However, although I found that I seemed to be able to train a horse alright, I struggled with the business side of my operation. I found it difficult to present myself in a confident, business-like manner, to really believe in myself, or, importantly, to sell myself. And having started with no funds really, financially I was against the wall from day one. There would be the occasional gamble landed, and then things would be good for a while. But overall my career was a twenty-year roller coaster ride, with me clinging on, often by my fingertips, for no good reason really, other than sheer pigheadedness.

I endured the best part of a couple of decades as the busy fool. Working hard each day for little financial reward. In the earlier days, the glow of the fire, a hot whiskey by my side, a lit cigarette, and the program book before me was reward enough. But I wanted it all, and I couldn't have it. And I didn't know it. I could train a horse. But that wasn't enough. I didn't know the game or how to play it. The game of life. I was brought up in a working-class household without my father. I just got on with it.

And so, over time, I began to consciously acknowledge something that I had felt intuitively for a long time. That maybe I didn't really belong here in Newmarket, maybe even in England. I had ambition, but lacked the confidence, the polish necessary to move comfortably with the moneyed racing set. A long-deceased, New York bricklayer father and an Irish mother who taught step-dancing was not the pedigree of successful Newmarket racehorse trainers. That was simply how it was, and I was the fool for carrying on and not taking it into consideration. Newmarket was where the establishment trained, and I was not a part of it. Or at least, that was how I felt.

And then along came Jack, like a parable. The son paying the sins of the father. His heart set on being a jockey.

There is a feeling, crouched low into a Thoroughbred at a gallop, that only those who have done it will really know. The exhilaration. Feeling at one with the world. The pair of you, bonded in the primal pleasure of just being. And when you dismount, you are walking tall, feeling light, your soul filled, other problems petty, other people slow and timid and nervous and afraid. As you yourself were, before you could do

15

this thing. And for some people, when they have experienced that feeling, they become hooked on it, and on the horses that make them feel that way.

So, I suppose I was woken from my sleepwalk through life by my son's dream. Should I continue to encourage him to plug away in Newmarket, one of thirty apprentices around town, all hoping for rides, while his heart was set on becoming an apprentice "bug boy" jockey in the States? Or should I get off that couch, book us our tickets, and head off for the promised land of America, where all you need is a good attitude, a willingness to work, and a belief in the American way, to at least be given a chance of succeeding!

At least, that is what I had been preaching all those years. Now, I wasn't so sure. Like the prisoner released after a lifetime of incarceration, I had grown fond of my cell. I had my certainties. The near certainty of ultimate failure that all except the most optimistic small-time trainers in Newmarket carry with them. The comfortable couch, with my comforting fire, in my cold but familiar home, where we had lived for the best part of twenty years. All of this I would have to give up, for what? Hope? Dreams? Success? Money? All of a sudden, it seemed like a bad deal to me.

But I had to do it. I had to do it because I had become resigned to my modest situation. I had to do it because I had told all that America was the answer, even if, deep down, I didn't really believe it. I had to do it because I was going nowhere—down to a few horses and no prospects of any more.

Mostly, though, I had to do it because I still, somewhere, had some fight, some spark left inside me. Not much, and not for much longer I could sense would it be there. But for now, there was still something. And I felt I had to either fan the spark, or let it fade and die. So, the question was, should I let what little we had slip away, in order to try to help our son achieve his dream, and maybe even get a second shot myself?

On August 18, 2014, Vicky, Jack, and I—and Geri the cat—boarded a Virgin Airways 747 from Heathrow Airport in London to JFK in New York. The same airport my mother had flown us out of forty-three years previously to come to England.

The news headlines that day were full of warnings about a possible imminent terror attack targeting flights to and from the USA, and the Ebola threat from passengers arriving at Heathrow from Africa. *Give me a break,* I thought.

Chapter 2

New York to Kentucky

I was five years old when our mother flew myself and my siblings out of John F. Kennedy airport in New York. Now I was forty-eight, and my son was eighteen. But I was here again.

When I stepped out of the airport terminal I was hit by the long forgotten, sickly-sweet mix of intense sweaty heat, stewing and brewing the smells farted from every building and passing vehicle that fills the spaces in cities like this in the summer. I like the stench of airports. The waft of aviation fuel, the whiff of human ingenuity, and the human urge to travel, to explore.

I don't understand it when people bellyache and moan over minor delays or small discomforts when flying. Air travel has changed the nature and direction of civilization. It has made gods of us all. Hurtling through the stratosphere at five hundred miles an hour, sat in a chair, tens of thousands of feet above the ground, just a paper-thin aluminium hull between us and six miles of fresh air. Puny humans, striding halfway around our planet in one day.

Yet, instead of marvelling that they are flying above the clouds. and gazing out at the skies and wondering at it all, appreciating that they are doing something men must have dreamed about forever, since they first saw winged birds. Instead, people moan about legroom, or their seat won't recline, or their potatoes are cold. It makes you think.

I pondered this, while, like a cliché, a yellow taxi took me and our bags to our hotel, whilst Vicky and Jack collected Geri. After I had checked in, I strolled across the road to a little bistro, sat outside, and had a beer in New York City.

Before I arrived, I had wondered whether I would get a feeling that I had come home somehow. Whether there would be some sense of returning, of belonging. After all I had been born just nineteen miles from the Empire State Building, which was just a big pitcher's throw from where I sat now. But I didn't. I felt like a tourist, a visitor, a stranger in someone else's town. I didn't mind that. After Newmarket, where everyone in the racing business knows everyone else, it felt nice to walk around a place and be a complete stranger. I have always liked the anonymity a city gives you.

The following day we awoke refreshed, and after breakfast headed off on foot to explore the Big Apple. We did the usual things. Selfies from the top of the Empire State Building, lunch in Central Park, and some shopping. It was fun, and it was nice to do normal family stuff—with no horses involved. And I was pleased that I could say, at last, that I had seen something of the city I was born in.

We went back to the hotel early that evening, picking up some large slices of pizza on the way, and contemplated our next task; driving from Manhattan, New York, to Lexington, Kentucky—via a quick trip to Boston to visit my cousin.

"It didn't look like much on the map," I mumbled to the family as they realized I had just added four hundred miles onto our trip to Lexington.

Boston was good, and it was great to see my cousins again, to see family. And we had more pizza—I was starting to worry our trip might undo Jack's career before he got started here. Jumping from a strict diet and sixty-hour weeks of hard physical labour to no work and a pizza-only diet could spell disaster for an aspiring jockey. I was beginning to imagine us arriving in Lexington with our rather obese, potbellied apprentice in tow.

The following day, after our goodbyes, we set off, on a road-trip of sorts. Heading into the unknown. Just the three of us, and the cat. Nine hundred and twenty-four miles and seven states, according to Google maps. Not around the corner, but by American standards not eyebrow raising, and I was planning an overnight stop.

I thought there might be something a bit more exciting and interesting about our journey, but it was just highways, and trees, and gas stations. After a long day of driving, I finally pulled off the interstate and into a place called Morgantown in West Virginia. We had covered six hundred miles, so were two thirds of the way to our destination. We booked into a hotel, I got a six-pack of beer, and we ordered our third pizza in as many days. I have no idea why sitting down all day is so tiring, but it is.

The next morning, we were off early, hotfooting it on our final leg, only a few hundred miles left. It felt like nothing after our journey the day before. And by early afternoon we entered Kentucky.

The Commonwealth of Kentucky is situated in the eastern third of the United States, and about midway between north and south; it is sometimes described as the most northerly southern state, or the most southerly northern state. Even during the Civil War they struggled to make up their mind. Horse farms are big here, of course, but so are tobacco farms and tobacco smoking. Lots of people smoke here. It was strange after coming from England, and I didn't really expect it in the United States. But when you get to Kentucky you realize that Britain really is a nanny state.

Smoking is cheap here. Four dollars a pack. I almost regretted having given it up. I suppose it whiles away the hours while driving. But I soon discovered Kentuckians have many ways to divert themselves whilst on the road.

Their favourite thing by far, I soon realized, is talking and texting on their phones. I am not referring to the furtive five-second phone calls people may take while driving back in the UK, or the two-word text responding to an urgent message received. No. I am talking about expansive discourses on the meaning of life, the universe, and every-thing, seemingly taking place in every other car, truck, and horsebox we passed in Kentucky. Hours long conversations that leave the driver so immersed they don't notice they are drifting across lanes, narrowly avoiding (and sometimes not) a fellow driver, also rapt in conversation, drifting the other way.

Often the drivers will be smoking, and they almost certainly will have a beverage in hand too. One young man passed us on the interstate, doing over seventy mph, with his bare foot extended out of the driver's window, while happily talking away on his phone.

I suppose it might not be so bad if there were safety barriers. But mostly there aren't. If you drift more than a couple of feet over the white line in many places here, then you are over the lip of the road and heading down a grass verge that sometimes may descend twenty or thirty feet quite precipitously. By the time your car has finished somersaulting down it your conversation will be well and truly over.

What they do have in place of safety barriers are adver-tising billboards. Most feature lawyers imploring you to call them if you, or someone close to you, has been involved in a wreck. These must be the richest people in Kentucky. If I start training again, these are the people I want to train for.

At a conservative estimate, about a third of all the cars in Kentucky seem to have dents in them. And the others, I assume, are just waiting their turn. Some just have a prang in the bumper, but others drive by so deformed that they are the mechanical equivalents of the Elephant Man. I have passed cars without grilles, without hoods, without doors. Without most things you would imagine people would like in a car. But does it stop them talking on the phone? Does it hell.

You see, this is the land of the free, and I think I am starting to get a feel for what that means now. You see, "free," here, seems not so much to mean, "you can't tell me what to do!" It seems more that "you can't tell me what *not* to do!"

Want to text friends on your phone while doing seventy-five on the interstate? Go ahead! Why should we put up safety barriers… Want to smoke three packs a day? Be our guest! No big government warnings here. No education, no job, like getting drunk and smoking some pot? Well, why shouldn't you have an AK-47 too! Shame on anyone who tries to deny you your freedom!

Don't want to wear a helmet while riding your motorbike—even though that truck driver is doing nearly eighty behind you, and he's on the phone, and smoking a cigarette, and been having chest pains but can't see a doctor, because no one's going to force him to have medical insurance. Well, that's your right to be free!

This is going to take some getting used to, I thought, as we drove into Lexington.

Chapter 3

The Bug Year: September 2014

Indiana Grand, Belterra Park, Kentucky Downs, Churchill Downs

The afternoon we drove into Lexington, we were on the ring road, circling, looking for a hotel to book into. So, when we saw a Comfort Suites hotel we pulled off at the junction. It was in a place called Beaumont, about fifteen minutes southwest of downtown. It was a fairly new area. Clean, well-kept, and suburban, with some nice restaurants. We liked it. And we stayed at that hotel for a month. And when it was time to find an apartment we found one at a nice complex just around the corner. And it became our new home, just like that.

It was trainer Jimmy Corrigan who got Jack going in Kentucky. We had only been in Lexington two days, our bags still unpacked, living in the hotel.

Jimmy has been in the USA since the 1980s, but his chirpy Irish accent would make you think he just arrived yesterday. He houses his string of horses at the Thoroughbred Center in Lexington, and, after an introduction, he kindly invited Jack to start exercising some of his horses for free in the morning.

Jimmy quickly became our friend, and our go-to person for sound advice. And I soon began to realize that his barn was doubling up as an unofficial branch of the Irish embassy.

We had assumed it would take a month or two before any offers of race-rides came, but within a few weeks of exercising his horses, Jimmy offered Jack his first mount stateside, at Indiana Grand Racetrack.

Then, just two days after that, he was booked for another ride at Belterra park in Ohio, and only a couple of days later, he found himself riding in an eighty-thousand-dollar maiden race at Kentucky Downs for another Irish trainer, Andrew McKeever - A man known to his friends as "The Bull" for his full-on personality. He spends his time stomping and roaring and cussing and is good fun.

It was after riding track work for The Bull one morning, that Jack got in the car and told me his old boss from Newmarket, Sir Mark Prescott—one of Newmarket's most renowned trainers (who was in town for a big bloodstock sale)—had been on the track apron with Andrew and watched Jack breeze (gallop) a horse.

"Really?" I said, quite excited. "What did he say?"

"He said, 'Good morning, Jack,'" said Jack.

"And what did you say?" I enquired.

"I said, 'Good morning, sir,'" he answered.

And that was it. So, I steered the car out of the backstretch to head home, a little nonplussed.

I was waiting to pull out onto the road, when Jack muttered darkly under his breath. "I didn't think I'd be seeing him again..." And we left it at that.

A fortnight later Jack made his debut at Churchill Downs. And then, a week after that, on September 27, 2014, on his ninth ride in North America, he tasted victory. His first winner in the United States! Belterra Park was the racetrack, and Aleutian Queen was the gallant filly!

That first win in the USA was significant for Jack in more ways than one. Apprentice jockeys all over the world claim a weight allowance to reduce the weight their horse is set to carry, in order to encourage trainers to utilize their inexperienced services. But the conditions of these claims vary from country to country. In the United Kingdom, a rider starts his or her career with a seven-pound weight claim, and this goes down in increments to five pounds and then three pounds, according to the number of winners they have ridden, until they ride their ninety-fifth winner when their claim disappears and they are deemed professional jockeys.

In the United States, a rider claims ten pounds until they have ridden five winners. Then their claim reduces to seven pounds, and from that point they have only twelve months until their claim is finished—whether they have ridden one winner or several hundred in that period. So there is no time to be wasted during an apprentice year in North America.

The reason apprentices in the States are known as "bugs" by the way, is down to the way the three levels of claim—ten pounds, seven pounds, and then after the fortieth win, five pounds, are denoted in the race programs by ***, **, and *. These asterisks next to the rider's name struck someone a long time ago as looking like a little bug on the race card—and so the term was born.

Aleutian Queen was Jack's first win stateside, but he had ridden four winners in the UK prior to arriving in North America, so she was his fifth career win, and therefore it triggered the start of his "bug" year. So, now the clock was ticking. And for the next twelve months, every single day, and every single mount would count.

That first win coming so quickly was a tremendous lift and a great relief. And I took it as hopefully some sign that maybe we were making the right move. It had been the best start we could have hoped for, and we felt prematurely vindicated that our American venture was unfolding just as we had envisioned!

Racing is a great leveller though. And everyone involved in the sport knows it is a game of constant ups and downs, sometimes literally.

It was the last day of the month, just three days after Jack's win. Vicky and I were down in the sports bar at Indiana Grand, situated inside the huge casino building behind the racetrack. The boy had a ride later in the day, and we were having lunch with Jack's newly appointed agent.

On the big screen on the wall they were showing the racing, and we could see a horse misbehaving in the paddock before its race. The horse threw the rider off, and he remounted. But then, when they eventually got it onto the track, it took one look at the lead pony and reared and flipped over and threw him again. And that was it. The jockey got up, thankfully okay, walked over to the horse, pulled his saddle off, and marched away in fear and disgust.

Now I had never seen this happen before. In the UK, unless the horse is withdrawn by the stewards or the vet, then the rider is expected to stick with it—no matter how hairy the experience! So, I mentioned this to the agent, and he explained that a rider can call off at any time if they are not happy, even at the starting gate. And, at the discretion of the stewards, the rider who calls off can also be replaced by another rider, even at this late stage—if anyone wants the mount.

"But who would be daft enough to offer to ride that?" I asked, laughing, just as the racetrack announcer called out that horse number seven would now be ridden by Jack Gill—

Vicky was out of the restaurant before the commentator had finished calling his name, and I wasn't far behind! It took a couple of minutes to get out onto the track apron, and I arrived just in time to see the horse rear over and flip Jack onto the outside rail. He bounced off it and got up, his thigh obviously a bit sore. But, before I could reach him, he was back up on the nag. The horse shied away from the lead pony again, but then, with his adrenaline up, Jack had had enough of its nonsense. He closed his legs on it, and with a crack of his stick down the shoulder, sent it forward, and the pair of them made their way, in haphazard fashion, toward the start.

The horse was pretty good at the gate—only throwing him off once. But the stall handlers got it in, and it jumped out, more or less, with the others, and the race itself went without event.

When he returned we met with him. Three pale faces together, and we asked him what he was thinking taking the ride.

"Well," he said, "someone came in the jockeys' room and asked if anyone wanted to pick up a mount. I was the only one about, so I said sure. They didn't tell me it was in the current race and had already dumped its jockey twice!"

So, Vicky and I went back down to the restaurant, and she had a big piece of chocolate cake to comfort her, and I had a large strong one to comfort me. And Jack learned to beware when strangers came offering gift horses…

September total: 1 win from 12 rides
Bug Year total: 1 win 12 rides

Chapter 4

Donning the Silks

It was Jimmy Corrigan who gave Jack his first horse to exercise in the USA. And he was the first trainer to give him a ride in a race here.

Elmor was the horse, a solid five-year-old gelding in a claiming race at Indiana Grand Racing and Casino. Jack had only been riding out for a couple of weeks at this stage of our American odyssey, and we had thought it would take a few months before any offers of rides came in. He had, however, obtained his apprentice jockey's license in the state of Kentucky a few days earlier, so we thought we were good to go.

In the USA, however, riders and trainers are licensed on a state by state basis. So, his apprentice jockey license in

Kentucky was not valid in Indiana, but getting the initial license was straightforward and had only cost around eighty dollars, so we weren't sweating it.

Indiana is not a place most Europeans would have probably heard much about. It lies directly to the north of the western half of Kentucky, and the racetrack itself is around a two-and-a-half-hour drive from Lexington, which is far enough (around 170 miles), but driving the 100 miles to Kempton Park racecourse from our stables in Newmarket often felt like more of a journey due to the weight of traffic and frequent jams. We have done the Indiana journey many times now, and it is not unusual once we have departed the Lexington ring road to not have to slow down, much less stop, until we reach the racetrack at Indiana. That is how smoothly traffic generally flows in these parts.

This part of Indiana is generally unremarkable. On our journey down to Lexington from Boston we drove through West Virginia for a couple of hours. Well, that was a couple of hours of looking at nothing but rolling hills densely covered in trees. Indiana is a bit like that, but without the hills and the trees. Flat level fields for mile after mile, punctuated with the odd religious banner (repent your sins).

Eventually we reached the racetrack. The whole area, for miles around, was flat, very flat. You don't really get places like it in England, not on this scale. Structures in the distance were a disturbance. It felt like you were missing a dimension.

Our first job was to get Jack licensed to ride, so we headed off to the racetrack office, for what I thought would be a formality.

I got a bad feeling the minute we walked in there. It was like a scene from some American movie. Some half-assed '70s style office, the exterior built from cinder blocks, the interior the recycled set of police headquarters from some old cop show. There were two girls manning the reception, and I could tell from their passive-aggressive smiles that there was going to be a problem. I don't know if it was the nerves of Jack about to have his first ride stateside, or if it was the slight hangover I was nursing. (I had discovered a store called the Liquor Barn across the road from our hotel, and, feeling anxious about Jack's upcoming ride, I had maybe overindulged.) Or, perhaps it was just the alien surroundings. But whatever the cause my pulse was starting to race, and I was feeling a bit edgy.

"Can I help you?" one of the girls enquired unhelpfully.

"I have a ride here today, and I need to get licensed," Jack offered.

"Have you been licensed before?" she replied.

"Yes, in the UK, and I have just got my Kentucky license."

"Okay, well, we need you to fill in this form, and then we will need your fingerprints, and we will also need documentation from the UK authorities, confirming you held a license there."

"Well, we have a letter of clearance from the British Horseracing Authority, which we presented to the Kentucky

33

Horse Racing Commission, who also fingerprinted him when they granted him his license," I interjected.

"We need to fingerprint him, and we need documentation sent to us from the UK authorities," she repeated as if she hadn't heard me.

"Well here," I said, "this is the letter." And I offered her my phone, on which I had opened the email with the letter of clearance that I had received from Joanne Crawforth at the BHA.

"We need the documentation sent to us." She smiled, declining to even glance at the phone.

"That's fine," I said, "can I use your Wi-Fi?"

"We don't have Wi-Fi," she said happily.

I tried to ring the BHA. It was 11.15 a.m. in Indiana, 4.15 p.m. in London. Jack's ride was less than three hours away, and the BHA people normally knock off at 5 p.m. sharp. There was no signal.

"We don't get a signal in here," she chortled. "You have to go outside." There was no signal outside. I went back inside.

"Look, I have a letter of clearance from the British Horseracing Authority, and he is licensed to ride as a jockey in Kentucky, and they have already fingerprinted him."

"We need the documentation sent to us," she cooed.

"Is there someone in charge here?" I said, exasperated.

"I am in charge of licensing," said the girl serenely.

"I need to speak to someone with authority, I have clearance from the UK but you won't look at it, he is already licensed in Kentucky, he has already been fingerprinted, this is ridiculous!"

I was starting to suspect all was not right here. The office didn't seem right; it was bare, like it had just been thrown together ten minutes ago. These people didn't want us here, we were interrupting something. There was something wrong with these girls with their fixed smiles. They were acting like androids with their scripted responses. No Wi-Fi, no phone signals…I don't know if it was the Grey Goose, but I was getting spooked. And then they brought out the steward, and I really started freaking out!

The girl shuffled out first, into the office from some back room, all blouse and painted smile, though even more forced now. Behind her emerged a man, Spanish looking, neat, with a perfect moustache, and dressed immaculately in a dark suit with a white shirt. He was very small. But slightly sinister. And he spoke in a whisper, like the chief of police in the '80s cop show *Miami Vice*—and that is who, I think, he reminded me of.

Once I had taken a moment to adjust, I explained the problem. He looked me sombrely up and down, for a long time, then he whispered seriously, "We are going to need a list in writing of all the horses he has won on, and the dates, and the racetracks too." I nearly combusted there and then. If I had still been smoking I would have had at least three alight in my mouth, whilst igniting a fourth. It was gone 4.40 p.m. London time. As he began to walk away, I interrupted him and begged him to please try and call Joanne Crawforth at the BHA and speak to her, and I gave him their number.

Reluctantly, it seemed, he agreed. And I prayed Joanne was there, as there was no time left otherwise to explain the situation and get the documents sent in time for Jack to ride.

By the time he came back out, the licenser had received a copy of the official letter of clearance from Joanne at the BHA, and she had also quickly typed up and included a list of Jack's four winners to date.

At that moment, I had never been so homesick for England. There, in the harsh Midwestern sunshine, in the flatlands, surrounded by hundreds of miles of flat fields, in some sparse office, with a sinister looking steward, all I could think about was England, the sweeping heath of Newmarket, damp mornings, London buses, HP sauce—Winston Churchill! And the British Horseracing Authority! Had there ever been a finer institution? Joanne's crisp British efficiency left me weeping for what we had left behind.

How could I have harangued, and railed against them, and not appreciated them for what they were when I was there? How my eyes had been opened. I was born again! An instant convert. The BHA was my church now, and Joanne Crawforth my patron saint!

So, Jack got his license. And he rode out onto the track for the first time in the United States of America and paraded with the other horses and riders as the bugler called them to post.

Elmor broke a bit slow in the race and was sitting midfield as the horses came around the turn and headed up the home stretch in virtual silence (to say the crowd was sparse would be like saying Lady Godiva dressed immodestly—there was no crowd), and as the field sped past me to the winning post, all you could hear was the thunder of hooves and the thwack, thwack of the jockeys' whips against the horses' hides. They finished last but one.

After pulling up, the pair of them turned and cantered back down the straight to unsaddle. They were both exhausted and caked from the top of Jack's cap to the tip of Elmor's hooves in thick dirt. He jumped off the muddy animal, and with weak arms, pulled his goggles down to expose a patch of clear skin around his eyes. And as he walked off with his saddle in his hand, his eyes glowed, and he shot us a smile as broad and pure as smiles come.

It was a good day to be in Indiana.

Disclaimer!

The office staff were, of course, polite and efficient and decent. And Jack has got to know and like very much the State Steward, who is a professional and a gentleman. In fact, we have invariably found the people we have had dealings with in the States to have been very courteous and accommodating. It is me who is the problem—I seem to have become prone to bouts of hysteria when stressed, and I was nervous about

Jack riding, so was emotional, and heck, it would have been boring otherwise…

Chapter 5

The Racetrack
Formerly Known as River Downs

Belterra Park is a new racetrack, opened only just before we arrived. But it is built roughly on the site of the old River Downs racecourse, a small venue in southern Ohio dating back to 1925. River Downs's biggest claim to fame possibly, is that it was where the legendary Steve Cauthen rode his first winner and where he launched his career. Well, its replacement was the venue that gave Jack Gilligan his first winner in the United States.

The track itself has no pretensions to greatness, the stands are modest, but like a lot of modest things it is likeable. Small and compact, with low grade racing mainly. But friendly and clean, with good food, and pleasantly situated beside the Ohio River, with a pretty, wooded hilly vista beyond the track.

The filly who gave Jack that first winner, was trained by Jeremiah O'Dwyer. He was in his first season as a trainer, and this was in fact to be his first winner too. Jerry previously rode a fair bit in the UK, and I knew him from his time in Newmarket. He was great to Jack from the start and helped and advised him a lot. So, when Jack sailed past the winning post lengths clear of the field, it was surprising to some that Jerry was in McCarthy's Irish Bar in downtown Lexington, watching a hurling match from back home. The filly was bet down to favourite before the off though. So, I knew he was there in more than just spirit...

For Jack, it was a big day. He'd said that his first ride at Indiana a couple of weeks earlier had felt slightly surreal, especially during the post parade, after a childhood spent watching and re-watching the Seabiscuit movie (incidentally Seabiscuit himself raced twice at River Downs—finishing third both times). And now here he was in the silks, astride the steaming beast. In the winner's enclosure! The genial commentator had done his homework and announced to loud and good-natured cheers from the crowd that this was, "Jack Gilligan's first win in the USA!"

It was a great feeling for me. Vicky was wearing a huge smile. We were both mightily relieved. It was not a small thing to leave our home of so many years and come to America. It had taken a toll on us already, and we hadn't exactly arrived at JFK airport stumbling out of first class and into a waiting limousine. So, for Jack to have ridden a winner within a few weeks of arriving in Kentucky was a better start than we could have hoped for. And, although a long way from a total vindication of our move, it did give us some comfort, some hope, some feeling of justification for doing what we did.

For me, I felt so pleased driving on to Indiana where he had another ride that evening, so relieved. So happy for Jack, who had worked so hard to be able to get to this point. And for some reason I thought about my own father, whom I had hardly known, and Jack had never even came close to meeting.

I know, now that I am a father, that a boy needs his dad. I don't think he really needs him to change nappies, or to burp him, or to feed him. I don't think those are things fathers are really necessary for. I think fathers are needed for guidance, for the transition from boy to man. For encouragement, for support, for advice, for criticism at times. For an arm around the shoulders in failure and for a quiet hug in victory. I think a father wants his son to succeed more than anyone else. For there is misery in failure.

I wanted Jack to succeed because I had tasted failure too much, and failure is bitter and sour on your tongue. And it makes life taste bad.

So it is my job, I feel, to try and help my son succeed. But I don't mean just winning. "Winning" is temporary, a fleeting thing, a trivial thing, really. One day you win, another you lose. Success lies in living well, seizing the day, remembering family and friends. Trying to have order and balance in life, having work that satisfies but doesn't consume, having some money in your bank account and friends to see. I think now, after a half century of consideration, that if you are good and lead a good life then you will gain much from even the smallest pleasures in this world. But if your life is led in a way that creates havoc, then only the big wins will bring respite, and even then, only fleetingly. For as I say, winning itself is temporary.

And so, that is why I think a boy needs his father. Because I tell him about things I think, like this, daily. Without thinking really and without having ever had anyone to tell me these things myself. And having not been told, I never lived like that, and never thought about those things until Jack was a young man. Until I could see he needed some guidance. And then I belatedly realized—unfortunately for him, probably—that, for better or worse, the job fell to me.

Chapter 6

The Bug Year: October 2014

Belterra Park, Mountaineer, Keeneland, Indiana Grand

October picked up where September had left off, with two winners the first week of the month back at Belterra Park, where now the commentator was calling Jack Gilligan home as "the hot bug!"

But then, just as he was getting going, the winners stopped. With hindsight, the tide maybe started to turn just a couple of days after his second win of the month, when we undertook the arduous six-hundred-mile round trip journey to Mountaineer racetrack in West Virginia, for one mount. When you go that far to ride a horse, you really need a winner

43

to set you up for the journey home; it didn't, and we have not been back since.

But then it was Keeneland. What a place it is! If you bring a friend to the races at Keeneland, and they don't like it, then get another friend.

I have not had a chance to visit Saratoga yet, but Claire-fontaine in Normandy, France, is very pretty indeed. And Leopardstown in Ireland is good. Del Mar in California is very fine, and Newmarket's July course takes a lot of beating. And little tracks like Salisbury and Ripon and Chester back in England are all charming too. But Keeneland, when the weather is right, is maybe the most pristine, the most beautifully manicured. The slickest show, the friendliest, the jolliest, the cleanest. It is probably as satisfying a tapestry of a racing day as you can get.

There are other tracks bigger and more impressive. Some better in some ways, several more important. But when you take the whole experience into account, it is very hard to beat. For me, it is a perfect boutique racetrack. Just the drive in, in the autumn, is perfect, the parklike approach with the trees resplendent in incredible shades of reds and oranges and rusts and pinks so intense and gorgeous, wrapping the whole facility in a cloak of many splendoured colours.

Unfortunately, however, it turned out that we were a lot more excited about Keeneland than it was about us. Jack, being just an inexperienced apprentice, was not likely to get many live mounts at the meet—especially being so new and unknown on the circuit. But even so, we hoped for a little better. In the end, a solitary fourth place from thirteen rides was the best he could muster through the month-long meet. We weren't disappointed though, because it was great to be there. And for Jack, just eighteen years old, in the country only a matter of weeks, to be riding against the best riders in North America—because for Keeneland the elite riders from New York and California fly in too—it was a tremendous experience.

It was nice also that Keeneland is in Lexington, and the small cosy apartment we had found to call home for a while was only a five-minute drive from the track. The mileage we were doing had come as a shock to us, and meant I was pretty much tied up as Jack's chauffeur, which we hadn't anticipated before our arrival. The devil is always in the details, isn't it?

Without the travelling, we had more free time to explore a bit of Lexington. We went to the movies, found a very good local Indian restaurant, which pleased us very much. We were able to find our feet a bit, and the more we saw, the more we liked it.

The University of Kentucky is based in Lexington, and that, together with Keeneland and its associated bloodstock auction house, make it feel quite a cosmopolitan, happening city. It seems cleaner, more prosperous, and more upbeat than the larger, but more grittily urban, Louisville, seventy miles away.

The people of Lexington have a well-deserved reputation for friendliness. And we found nearly everyone to be very polite, open, and helpful. So, I had to quickly try and brush off my rough edges! It is a very civilized place on the whole, and the suburban middle classness of Beaumont, where we lived, was a refreshing change from Newmarket, a rowdy town of blue collars and blue bloods.

By the end of the month though the bug was hungry for another win or two. He picked up ten rides for the last few days of the Indiana meet, which yielded three seconds, but no victory. And so, he finished the month with just the two wins from forty-five rides. Not a disaster, but a couple of quick winners would help, as trainers and owners pay close attention to a rider's statistics here, so maintaining a decent strike rate was important.

October total: 2 wins from 45 rides
Bug Year total: 3 wins from 57 rides

Chapter 7

If Hell Has a Racetrack, It Will Be Called Mountaineer

I t began, innocently enough, with John. He was one of many Irish expats training small squads of horses around the training centres of Lexington. Some had come here openly, some under cover of darkness, but good men all. They embraced Jack from the start and supported him with rides.

So, John mentions a horse he shall be entering for the following week. "It's at Mountaineer," he mentions casually, "bit of a way, but I think it will win."

"That's great," I blurt out, "we'd love to ride it." No sooner had I said it, than I knew the game was afoot. I had trapped myself. John allowed himself a satisfied smile.

Now, I knew Mountaineer Casino Racetrack and Resort was not around the corner, but when I checked the route and discovered that you wouldn't get much change out of six hours each way, I started to regret my enthusiasm.

Over the following days, news began to spread amongst the rest of the gang that we were to attempt Mountaineer. Jimmy, who has been training horses around these parts for thirty years, didn't pull any punches. "I went there once, never again. It was like being in another country," he said, in tones that suggested he was still trying to come to terms with the experience. "It was like we'd left America."

That seemed to be the general attitude of most people we discussed it with. But I had made an agreement—and Jack was going to honour it! So, we got our travel bags prepared, and I booked us in for a night at the Mountaineer Casino, Racetrack and Resort hotel.

Jack had a few to breeze the next morning, and that all went smoothly. The sky was overcast, and we were expecting some rain on the journey, but my spirits were high. Just the three of us on a little American road trip. It would be fun, and hopefully Jack could have a winner. As we were getting ready to depart from the trainer's barn he flagged us down. "They say you shouldn't drink the water there, you know, something to do with industrial pollution." And with that, we were on our way.

The route, like most routes across the States, was straight-forward enough. There are times at junctions when it's easy enough to go wrong, but mostly you're just cruising along. We took the 75 north to Cincinnati, a route we knew well and liked, as it was the road we took to Belterra Park, where all three of Jack's wins to date had come. The nice little track, situated "by the banks of the majestic Ohio!" as the entertaining commentator there would boom during the course of most races.

Our route took us straight through the heart of the city on an overpass. Cincinnati has its skyscrapers, and I would describe it as a bit Gotham city like, but we were pedal to the metal through it. And then we took the 71 northeast to Columbus and so far, so good.

Then it began to rain. It wasn't too bad at first, but as we were heading toward Columbus I became aware that slowly everything was starting to blend into a shade of grey all around us. Ahead, the distinction between land and sky was becoming blurred. It was unusual, and the sky was getting darker and darker. And then we drove into it. The grey was not mist, or cloud, or even drizzle. It was rain so heavy and thick that visibility was instantly cut to, well, it felt like zero. I had trouble seeing which way the road in front went, even with my speed down to around twenty miles an hour. I know we think it rains in England, but I have never experienced anything like this. It didn't hit the windscreen like rain. It hit it like there were three or four people being fed buckets of water, which they continuously and simultaneously threw at my windscreen. This carried on for what felt like an hour, before eventually, to my great relief, it broke. And off we sped again, chastened, and a little unsettled. But soon we were in West Virginia.

There isn't really much I can say about West Virginia. But if you are a really big fan of trees, then come here, and you will think you have died and gone to heaven, because for a few hours that is pretty much all we saw. Lots and lots of trees. Then we started to race alongside the majestic Ohio, which was nice. And then we came upon the gates of hell...

Now, don't get me wrong, the gates of hell themselves weren't too awful, I am just referring to them as the point when we leave the trees behind, mostly, and approach the mining towns. Slices of mountain were cut away to our left for open-face mining, and to our right, beside the Ohio river, were huge heaps of glistening black coal piled impossibly high. Vast black rusted factories spewed stinking smoke from huge chimneys. A spaghetti array of pipeworks raced alongside the road on both sides of us, and every now and then one pipe would peel off over us and zip off to the other side of the road. Ugly, yes, and polluting, but for a long time, necessary, and functioning, and providing utility and employment, and energy for the nation.

The towns themselves started okay. But each one we drove through grew successively smaller and poorer looking and depressed. And you just knew things weren't going to be getting better anytime soon. Eventually however, the trees greeted us once more, and the road began to wind; it was winding all the way to Mountaineer.

Mountaineer racetrack is located beside the Ohio River. There isn't much else around, no sign of civilization really, just the road to Mountaineer and a strip joint. Yes. God help me, it's true. Here. Beyond the back of beyond, there was apparently a more pressing need for dancing girls than for pickup trucks, helicopters, or even hiking boots and survival equipment. And what manner of exotic creatures could be lurking within? I don't know. Jimmy claims that he went there once and offered the girls money to put their clothes back on, saying he just wanted a beer. But Jimmy claims a lot of things.

It was only a matter of yards from the concrete bunker that was the strip club to the entrance to Mountaineer, so I had not fully digested the visions dancing in my mind when I swung the car in and stepped onto the territory of Lucifer himself.

The weather didn't help, it was grey and drizzling. But it wouldn't have made much difference. When we got out of the car the air smelt off, which immediately explained why the racetrack owners decided not to name it Mountain Air, a more fragrant and seductive name indeed, but one even the execs' must have laughed hollowly about when plumping for its current label.

The hotel itself was big and new, with an impressively large marble foyer. There were food outlets in different trajectories and ahead of us was the sprawling casino. Don't think *Casino Royale* when you imagine this place though. There were some poker tables tucked away, but by far the biggest business of these racetrack casinos is slot machines. Banks and banks of them, hundreds and hundreds of them. Each one, seemingly, piloted by an elderly person, and, it seemed, most of them were smoking. The smell of cigarette smoke made everything seem old and sticky, even though it wasn't. It smelt stale; the poor people who were so hopelessly throwing their money away, they seemed stale. Did hell have a purgatory? Was this hell's waiting room? I needed a beer. And a chaser.

We whiled away the hours until the race in our hotel room, which actually was nice and clean and new. It is strange as an ex trainer just taking my jockey racing, a horse takes a lot more looking after before its race than a jockey, I can tell you that for nothing.

When the time rolled around we headed back out to the hotel car park. We could see the racetrack now, looming out of the black drizzle. The great spotlights were lighting the track and shadowing the imposing, if slightly sinister-looking glass and metal grandstand, which had, years ago, been built to a scale that could accommodate a positive throng. That was a mistake. The management could have imported one of our red telephone booths from England to satisfy all the demands of paying customers. There were no paying customers. Only the poor souls of horsemen and jockeys who must have, long ago, made a pact with the devil. And the devil had called his dues. So now they plied their trade throughout the meet, and stabled their equally damned horses there on the backstretch. And then there were people like us, walking around in a daze, first- and last-timers, who came to witness horse racing from hell.

When you think of a race paddock, I should imagine you think of an oblong or large circle, with white rails and bushes and green turf on the inner, and the owners and trainers chatting in the middle, whilst the horses walk proudly around.

Okay. You at least imagine it being outside, don't you? Not here. Think of a concrete cylinder with great holes gouged out of it, or saddling stalls, as they call them here, and on the outside of the walking ring another concrete cylinder to enclose the field. The horsemen are on the ground floor watching the horses circling in the jaundiced light, like some nightmarish carousel. The jockeys come out wearing not the proud owners' colours, but a primary colour dictated by the horse's post position. Spectators—assuming there were any—would need to lean over a balcony a floor above and look down—through netting—at the scene below. Dante missed this one.

Eventually, Jack's turn came, and we rushed through, along with the other connections, from the paddock, into the heart of the building, then up a floor, where we cut through the bar and betting outlet, and raced through the doors at the front, into the blackness of the night.

The rain still fell clearly through the spotlights, and the race was run. The filly was awkward at the start and broke slowly, and she was never a factor after that. Twelve hours for nothing in an instant. Well, what did you expect when you come to the devil's playground?

The next morning, as we were loading the car ready to leave, the sun was shining, and things looked a bit better, and on the way home I pondered why everyone was so down on the place. It really wasn't that terrible, and since it first opened in 1951, then known as Waterford Park, it had enjoyed times of popularity. And the little towns and the factories and the smells, well, there are worse things and places around.

After some consideration though, I came to this conclusion. I think it is this. This just isn't the place or the time for a racetrack. Racehorses are beautiful athletes. They shouldn't be adjuncts to a casino. They shouldn't be paraded inside, they shouldn't be racing at night, in the rain, in the middle of nowhere. And they shouldn't be asked to run themselves to exhaustion - when no one is even bothering to watch.

<u>*Chapter 8*</u>

And Then We Went to Keeneland

It is a bit corny, I suppose, to say that if Mountaineer racetrack is hell, then Keeneland must be heaven. But that is how it felt.

Keeneland saw its first day's racing on October 15, 1936, right in the middle of the Great Depression, which had occasioned the demise of Lexington's previous racing venue, the Kentucky Association racetrack.

The brainchild of prominent local horsemen Hal Price Headley and Major Louis Beard, the Keeneland track stands as a testament that great things can be achieved successfully, and sustained and improved on, without the relentless, mindless pursuit of profit maximization. The racetrack, and indeed the world's largest bloodstock auction house, which is now also part of Keeneland and intimately shares its grounds, are a not-for-profit venture. Profits realized are ploughed back into improvement of facilities, philanthropic deeds, and prize money.

Hal Headley said, "We want a place where those who love horses can come and picnic with us, and thrill to the sport of the Bluegrass. We are not running a race plant to hear the click of the mutuel machines. We want them to come out here, to enjoy God's sunshine, fresh air, and to watch horses race." They don't really make people like that anymore, do they?

Well, Mr. Headley, lay easy in your long good night. Because under the leadership of the twinkle eyed and eccentrically named Rogers Beasley, Keeneland is a place where everything is right. And I mean everything. It is so right, it could almost be a definition, a byword, a moniker of right, an appellation. A utopia.

Situated in rolling parkland on the western outskirts of Lexington, on land purchased from a Mr. Jack Keene, the long winding entrance road is immaculately tarmacked, and old-fashioned streetlamps line the route (by the way, whenever I talk about anything here, just throw in an "immaculate" for yourself to save me the job—the quaint green wooden benches, immaculate; the neatly pruned paddocks, immaculate; the catering booths selling premium hotdogs, Kentucky burgoo, and candy, immaculate; the bars selling bourbon cocktails, immaculate; the restrooms, you've got it, and they are too—even during racing).

As you drive in, trees are scattered across the parkland with leaves in every autumn hue of yellow and green and brown and rust and gold, and incredible reds of every shade, from delicate rose pink, to blood as dark and fresh as from an artery. Nature at its most beautiful. But helped along with a human touch, as these trees have arrived in their setting with the care one could ordinarily only expect of an actuary with obsessive-compulsive disorder. The result is prettier than nature alone could achieve, and as you approach the parking areas, you see the trees unite to stand in perfect lines, sheltering the cars from the sunniest days.

The grandstand itself is built from large, light grey blocks of Kentucky limestone, a tribute to the original stone barn that stood on Mr. Keene's land, giving it a slightly castle-like impression from the outside.

Entrance fees start at only a few dollars. And people flock here. Green-jacketed attendants at every entrance are shouting information, greeting and welcoming the people thronging in, ready to answer any questions they might have. The first area you come to is the paddocks. To the far end is where the horses are led around, waiting for the valets to bring out the saddles for their races. Once ready, they wait for the call to parade in the main ring, where the jockeys and trainers and owners meet. Towering above the ring is an imposingly large and beautiful silver sycamore. It stands there, like some oversized student of the form, its arms and hair wild in the wind.

Once the jockeys are mounted, the horses are led through an opening under the grandstand. They emerge into the sunlight and out onto the track to the poignant notes of the bugler.

Horses in North America don't have to be led to the start, but they generally are. The outriders at some tracks often look as if they have taken to sleeping rough, but here they are all in Keeneland green. It is a nice spectacle for a nice crowd. Most people here aren't huge race fans, but they don't ignore the racing: they read the *Form,* they look at the horses in the paddocks, and they bet their trifecta boxes, and their superfectas, and their pick sixes, and cheer as loudly as at any British track, which creates an atmosphere and energy often lacking at tracks stateside. And after the race is run, they turn back to their friends, for this is primarily a social gathering, a place to go and dress up and be seen. Blazers, bow ties, and cigars are the tradition for men. Ladies, anything from haute couture to casual. No one judges, it's just however you feel, and what the weather is like. Lots of people enjoy a drink, but everyone seems to conduct themselves well, even on the days with free admission for students, which was an eye-opener.

There are tracks in Britain and Europe as pretty, and there are some tracks that also offer the high levels of prize money. And there are some that you can enter without getting a payday loan. And there are some that are very clean, and some that offer good food and drink easily and not too expensively, and some even have that great mix of people having fun without getting too carried away, places where you could let children run off together and do their thing, allowing the adults to do theirs. But I can't think of another track that I have been to, that does all these things so well.

Keeneland is an example of American ambition when it seemed of a more noble kind, and is a shining example of American hard work and can-do attitude and efficiency, and all of the things that as a kid growing up, I imagined America to be. And have found, now that I have returned, that often, inevitably, it is not.

I suppose it is a bit like an English child brought up in America, imagining England's good manners, and dress, and civility, and cosy fires in country inns, and red buses, and telephone boxes. And then after many years, returning to find KFC, and Poundland, and tattoos and litter, and drunks everywhere, and traffic laced with snarling drivers… But still, here and there, the odd gloriously good pub.

Keeneland is good, its intentions are good, and its actions are good. And its execution is brilliant.

So, I can tell you now, and I am sure that I am the first. It is a mere six-hour drive from heaven to hell. So I beg you, please. Take careful heed in which direction you are headed.

Chapter 9

The Bug Year: November 2014

Churchill Downs

By November in the American Midwest, Indiana Grand in Indiana, and Belterra Park in Ohio have shut down for the winter, and only Churchill Downs in Kentucky remains open.

It is a bleak, undressed horse-racing scene at this time of year. Trainers are getting ready to send their strings of horses down to Florida, or Louisiana, or Arkansas for the winter. And the whole area feels like it is getting ready to hibernate. The sidewalks are blanketed with rusted leaves, and the trees are stark and naked. People are wrapped up bundles shuffling around the streets, and the sky alternates between a tepid faded blue and a colour-sapping grey. Days are generally cold now, and although racing is strictly business, not pleasure, at this time of year, this is still Churchill Downs, and there are still nice horses to ride in nice races with good purses. This is also the time of year when a two-year-old maiden race could throw up a monster, could introduce a greenhorn, young Thoroughbred debutant who, just twelve months later, could be an established star known throughout the racing world.

There was little chance someone would entrust such a potential star to the new bug boy. But still he was there. Sometimes riding a no-hoper in a fifty-thousand-dollar maiden race, sometimes riding something with an outside chance in a twenty-thousand-dollar claimer. He was there all month, gaining experience, getting cold, getting wet, getting dirt kicked in his face. He spent one night under the floodlights experiencing all of that multiple times. And I sat in the stands as the month wore on and watched, and wondered what the hell we had been thinking. And I grew more anxious and worried and depressed. And the weather began to match my mood well.

No one would put him on a horse with a live shot. The bigger trainers wouldn't even give him a chance to breeze for them in the mornings. "He's too tall," was the dismissive comment of many. Well he hadn't been too tall when he'd won by a nose, at 33/1, on the second ride of his life at Newbury Racecourse in Berkshire—every bit the equal of Churchill Downs prestige-wise. He wasn't too tall to notch up seven winners from his first forty-five mounts, for a very respectable lifetime sixteen percent strike rate.

I was cold, wet, worried, anxious, and scared. We were rapidly running out of money. Not an unfamiliar sensation for me, but one that had more sinister repercussions here. I had told Vicky before we came that I thought America was not somewhere I would want to be without cash in the bank. And nothing I had seen since we had been here had changed that opinion. There was no safety net here. And, of course, there were people on the sidelines—they are always on the sidelines, aren't they?—who would be happy to see our sojourn fail. That is just a fact of life.

Our apartment was rented. I had been renting a car for over three months. Everything cost money. I had furnished our apartment with a small outdoor picnic table and three folding canvas picnic chairs, which I picked up for next to nothing in an end-of-season sale at a Rite Aid store.

You may of course ask, dear reader, why, if I was going broke, didn't I get a job? And I am asking myself the same question right now… I suppose I could claim that, like De Quincey, it just never occurred to me…an ex-racehorse can be retrained perhaps, an ex- racehorse trainer, maybe not… But, more honestly, Vicky had taken a position with a local stud farm, and I was tied, very much, as a full-time driver—we'd had no idea of the mileage Jack would need to do on the Midwest circuit, but our expenses were very much exceeding our income. And I discovered driving my jockey didn't pay that well…

By the end of the month, from thirty-four rides—a respectable number considering it was Churchill Downs—Jack had notched up three second places, but not a single victory, and that meant his statistics going into the Turfway Park meet—which we had decided to stay for, instead of heading south for warmer climes, as many had advised—read three wins from ninety-one rides, which was, quite frankly, a disaster of *Titanic* proportions career-wise for Jack, and an insult to a rider of his talent and ability. A total of three winners when he was nearly twenty-five percent through his bug year was not something I had ever envisioned. But if the horse isn't quick enough, the jockey can't win on it. As Jack's legendary valet, the inimitable, Todd Taylor, told Jack after a trainer had chewed him out a bit after a race, "You tell 'em, when the horse starts running. I'll start riding!"

And so, Jack packed up his tack and sent it north to Turfway Park to embark on four months of night racing in the frigid, and increasingly bleak-looking, mid-winter of northern Kentucky, four thousand miles from home.

November total: 0 wins from 34 rides
Bug Year total: 3 wins from 91 rides

Chapter 10

The Bug Year: December 2014

Turfway Park

By the time we took the I-75 north for the seventy-eight mile journey to Turfway Park in Kentucky on the first Thursday of December, the American dream was turning very sour for me.

Jack was taking the lack of winners pretty well. He was young and busy doing his job each day, breezing in the mornings and at least getting rides—if not winners—in the afternoons, evenings, and now, nights.

On the plus side, he was certainly getting a lot more mounts than he would have been expecting at this stage of his career back in the UK. And there is usually no racing in

Kentucky or the surrounding states on Mondays, so the job is rarely seven days a week. And mucking out stables was a thing of the past for him now, which suited him just fine! Here in the States, the grooms muck out and tack up the horses, and the hotwalkers cool them off after exercise. So, Jack's job was literally just riding the horses, and even then, only in trial gallops, or "breezes." Exercise riders ride the horses on a day-to-day basis. And best of all, as far as he was concerned, was that his hands hadn't touched a broom since he'd left Sir Mark's! These were all splendid things to Jack, and I think he was happy to forego a few wins in order to enjoy this new pampered life.

But the clock was ticking away all the time, day in, day out, in the background. And his time to claim, his time to prove his worth as a rider, was slipping quietly away.

So, when we arrived at Turfway Park on the fourth of December, Vicky and I were full of trepidation, stressed and worried, for the first night of what could be four long months of winter racing. With the first race scheduled to go off after six p.m. every night except Sunday, and the last race not off till around ten-thirty p.m., it was going to be a lot of late nights, followed by long drives home, through the harsh winter, down dark highways, not getting home until well after midnight.

And then his first mount, on the first evening of the Christmas meet, won. And later that night he won another. And all of a sudden, Kentucky, and Turfway Park in particular, was just a great place to be!

A double, on the first day of the meet. And three days later he rode another double. And suddenly he was the hot bug once more! And just as the drought seemingly started for no good reason, it ended just as inexplicably, just as suddenly, just as unexpectedly.

And that's racing. And I should have known better, as during my own career I had on several occasions been drawn so low by my own results, only to be rescued from despair by a timely winner, the cure for all ills for jockeys and trainers. Our drug of choice.

And of course, success breeds success. Those four winners that first weekend meant that Jack's valuable claim was suddenly in demand for live mounts with favourites chances, and he didn't waste those opportunities now coming his way.

The following weekend yielded another double, and the week after that he bagged two more victories. And to cap off the year he rode his fourth double of the month on the day after Christmas.

In the end, he had ten winners from seventy-eight rides that December, which was more than most apprentices in their first full season back in the UK would get in a year.

And so, by the skin of his teeth, the year was saved. Honour was redeemed. The bug year was getting back on track, it was all still to play for, and he was entering the New Year on a roll!

Jack had ridden his first winner of the year, for me, back in April at Wolverhampton Racecourse on the outskirts of

Birmingham. He gained his sixteenth winner of the year in December at Turfway Park in Florence, Kentucky. In between he had experienced a lot and learned a lot.

Back in April Jack was still working for Sir Mark Prescott at the historic Heath House stables, in his hometown of Newmarket. It was a relentless diet of long hours mucking out stables, sweeping yards, and exercising the horses for Sir Mark and for me each morning, with a ride in a race coming maybe every week or two.

Having just finished school, Jack found the work and the hours very arduous. And they were. Sir Mark Prescott's yard is the tightest run ship in Newmarket, which was why I sent Jack there, and it is definitely not a place for the workshy. He had to be up just after four a.m. each morning, would gulp a few mouthfuls of porridge—which Vicky would force-feed him with his eyes still shut. And then he would stumble out of the house and around the corner to Heath House, looking like an underfed, overworked urchin heading to the workhouse. Which I suppose, in a way, he was.

And then in August, we came to America. His last ride in the UK was a winner at Great Yarmouth Racecourse, and he had just been starting to get going. Sir Mark liked Jack, and thought highly of him, and no doubt would have given him many good opportunities. But Jack wanted to try his hand racing in North America, and with the lower weights the horses carry stateside, we felt he needed to go soon, before he got bigger and stronger and heavier.

The first day I went with Jack to a training track in the USA and saw horses exercising, it was a shock, to be honest. If you like the Thoroughbred horse, then you will never find anywhere to match Newmarket Heath in the morning. The imposing strings of horses out at exercise, some of them forty or fifty strong, galloping across the ancient turf. Hundreds of miles of grass gallops, dozens of miles of artificial surfaces, each one carefully designed with the horses' soundness, and welfare, and training in mind.

But here it was different. The horses trained around an oval track. The surface is what they say it is, dirt. A dead, ugly surface, no spring in it to store potential energy in the tendons, to help the horse, not much thought of the horse at all, that I could see. I watched the horses' feet shear forward on landing in the mud, and I shuddered. Just training, day in, day out, around a left-hand oval would be enough to lame many young equines.

The horse has evolved over millions of years to escape its predators by running away fast, in more or less a straight line. Hares run in circles in nature. Horses don't. Their legs have not evolved for galloping at full speed around one hundred and eighty degree turns. And when you ask any machine to do something it is not really designed to do, and you push it to its limits, then eventually, it may break.

So, it was horse racing. But things were different, training regimes were different, the style of racing was different, the dirt surface was different, the views on how a jockey should look and ride were different. Gallops are timed by the quarter mile here, and so are races. Toe in the iron, sticks up, flat back, no bumping up and down in the saddle.

And Jack learned by getting stuck in, by jumping into it. And early on, sometimes he breezed them too slow, and the trainers—who, on the whole, were rather more restrained and polite than their Newmarket counterparts—would grimace and mutter under their breaths. And sometimes he would go faster than they'd like, and that would elicit the same response. But over time Jack started to get it right more and more often, and he clicked with some trainers and started to build up relationships with them, and I would listen to his assessments of horses and realize how much he was absorbing, how much he was learning, how far he was coming along. And I could see that by breezing maybe twenty or more horses every week, instead of a half dozen a week back home, that this was an intensive process.

Every horse he sits on in the USA he rides fast. I suppose it is the difference between a pilot and a test pilot. You need to think quicker, react quicker, do everything tighter, everything exact, everything right.

So, at the age of eighteen Jack now had considerable experience of racing in the United Kingdom and in North America. And that made him fairly unique. It had been arduous, tough. And for Vicky and myself, very emotional. But he had learned a tremendous amount in just a few months, and he had got his foot in the door of American racing. And so, as we sat down for Christmas dinner with new friends in Kentucky, we were missing home, but we weren't ready to go back yet. There was more to be done.

December total: 10 wins from 78 rides
Bug Year total: 13 wins from 169 rides

Chapter 11

The Poor Man's Wolverhampton

Opened in 1959 as Latonia Race Course, Turfway Park racetrack is situated on the outskirts of the town of Florence, which is located at the northernmost tip of Kentucky. In spirit though, the place is more akin to the rowdier city and state directly above it, and within spitting distance—Cincinnati, Ohio. When people ask me what it is like, I say it is like the poor man's Wolverhampton.

Entering the grounds of the racetrack, the grandstand looms surprisingly large and square, and a bit rusty, with the legend "Turfway Park" emblazoned across it in huge green lettering. Valet parking is offered, but since there are about ten acres of parking space and usually around sixty cars, it seems more modest to park oneself.

Entrance is free most days, as it is for many of the small tracks in the States. The ground floor is basically a betting shop, smoke filled, and replete with all of the odd, boisterous, pugnacious, clawing, fighting to stay ahead, to stay sane characters that are found in any betting shop in Britain. I liked it, it reminded me of my hometown of Newmarket—a bit seedy, with its share of chancers, and chasers, and triers.

On a Saturday night they have live music upstairs, and the people from Cincinnati come to unwind after a week's work, to drink, and bet, and dance, and laugh with their friends, and the place is rowdy and jumping and fun. And on Cincinnati Bengals game days half of the customers are dressed in bright orange football shirts, adding a certain prison chic quality to the place.

On the upper floors—all enclosed in glass to keep the bitterly cold Kentucky night at bay—one can drink beer (dollar dogs and beers on Friday and Saturday—what a deal! I recommend the beer, but would suggest stumping up a couple of extra dollars for a hundred-percent-beef, quality dog). There is also a Mexican food outlet, and various other vendors. Almost everything on offer is fried and brown but tasty, so what the heck. Trust me, your fellow patrons here are more of a risk to your immediate well-being than the chili cheese fries.

We normally take a table in the ground floor restaurant for racing. After the free entrance, the purchase of a blackened Cajun steak sandwich with fries, gives you a table for the evening. It is a non-smoking room, and there are a multitude of TV screens showing racing from tracks all around the country, as well as the big game if there is one on. The décor is basic, but the food is fine, the service is friendly, and the surroundings comfortable and warm; and we can easily make our way out to the paddock before each of Jack's races.

The paddock area itself is large and well presented, and in the run up to Christmas, they play seasonal music quietly in the background, which, with the snow and frost under the spotlights, is kind of surreal and nice.

The track at Turfway is not dirt as is normally the case in the US, but a synthetic surface known as Polytrack. The surface is old though, and its black colour is evidence of its degradation. And attempts to revitalize it seem to have been pretty limited. The kickback, which in the UK is minimal on these surfaces, is severe; the horses often don't face it, and Jack comes home with red welts on his arms, legs, and face, and sometimes cuts.

But he has no complaints, the breakdown rate for horses here is lower than at most tracks in the States, and Jack came to Turfway with three stateside wins to his name. On the first evening of the winter meet back at the beginning of December, he rode a double and proceeded to repeat the feat each of the next three weeks—rendering my Gilligan family record of three lifetime doubles to the wastebasket—in one short month. In the first ten weeks of racing he notched up twenty-two wins here. He also had a couple of places in stakes races, and a couple of weeks ago he rode a treble.

Now a double is something. It isn't easy, you know. I had three in sixteen years of training, and that wasn't bad since I only averaged a runner a week throughout my career. But even though Jack often rides six races on a card, there are up to thirty jockeys riding here on any given day, and there are only nine races. So, to win two of the nine leaves a lot of jockeys without a win. But to win three, well that is very hard to do—and he was only beaten a head in a four-way photo for a fourth win in the last.

That day, after he had washed and changed, he came out of the jocks room, and he was choked at not getting the fourth win. So, on the way home I told him this: "This was a big day for you today and you must savour that, and appreciate what you have achieved. Do not be in too much of a rush to your destination, take time along the way to enjoy the road and its scenery. And do not worry that you didn't win the last, for if you had won four today how do you top that tomorrow? What do you aim to achieve then? Now you will wake up in the morning happy at what you have done, but you will still have a hunger within you, urging you on, to improve, to do better, to do what you nearly did. To win four in a day."

And that is the jockey's life, even more than the trainer's. The trainer has a business to run, horses and staff to care for. Owners to deal with and bank managers to meet. Winners for most trainers are a relief, a lift, a sign to keep going. For a jockey, especially over here, it is a relentless, promiscuous notching of bedposts. Victory after victory, hardly time, it seems sometimes, to draw breath from one, before chasing the next. That is his job now, and he seems born to it.

And what did he make of my advice? Well, when I turned my head driving home in the dark to see what he thought of my wise words, he had his headphones on listening to music, and he was messaging his friends on Facebook.

Chapter 12

The Bug Year: January 2015

Turfway Park, Mahoning Valley

Earlier in 2014, while we were still in England, Jack had been chosen to represent Great Britain in the H.H. Sheikha Fatima Bint Mubarak Apprentice World Championship, a series of apprentice races taking place across the world with the final held at the Abu Dhabi racing festival. As a result of having taken part (he finished third in his race at Newbury), Jack had been kindly invited by the Abu Dhabi royal family to join them in the United Arab Emirates for their New Year's Eve celebrations, all expenses paid!

It was a difficult decision. And, not for the first time in mine, or now his career, I made the wrong one. I felt that now he had just got rolling here in America, that to take off on a jolly to the UAE for a week, instead of trying to kick home some winners at the start of the year, might rub some of his supporters the wrong way. Some people, especially in the racing industry, seem to think that the world won't keep spinning without them clocking in to work every day.

Well, they are wrong, and so was I. I advised him to stay, and he did. And on New Year's Day, on his second ride at bitterly cold Turfway Park, his mount reared up and flipped over in the gate. He was flung out the back, but his right foot got stuck in the stirrup iron, so he was left suspended—upside down, behind the gate, with his foot still attached to his saddle, which in turn was still attached to a half-ton Thoroughbred, which had found itself in a similarly undignified position still inside the gate.

I think a few things probably ran through Jack's mind at this time, such as: *Maybe I should look at something else to do for a living.* And: *I bet all the other apprentices are asleep in a luxury hotel right now.* And of course: *I really shouldn't listen to my father.*

The stalls handlers were brilliant. Two ran to Jack and raised him up, while a third pulled his foot out of the iron, and they carried him away from danger in a few seconds flat.

He was just about fine, but I had chosen a bad day to give up drinking. He didn't ride a single winner that week. And there is a moral to all that somewhere…

The second week of the new year provided a couple of winners, including the first of seven he was to win on a mare who would become a favourite to us all—Will Gracie Shine, a tough and honest little chestnut trained by North America's winning-most female trainer, Kim Hammond.

Weeks three and four each yielded a winner apiece, both times in more valuable thirty-thousand-dollar allowance races—which the jockey liked.

And then Jack's agent, for no apparent reason, booked him for one ride at Mahoning Valley Race Course and casino in Ohio.

Ohio is quite a long state north to south. About three hundred and sixty miles all told. Turfway Park is just over the southern edge of the Ohio state border. And Mahoning Valley is pretty much at its northern edge. In fact, when you have gone as far north in Ohio as you can, there is nothing but an invigorating swim in Lake Erie between you and Toronto.

Anyway, come the day I didn't need to go, as Mark the agent had volunteered to drive the 720 mile round trip. But it was an opportunity to visit another racetrack, and it was my mission to see as much of North American racing, and indeed North America, as I could. So I jumped in for the fun of it.

The furthest I ever drove in the UK in one day was from Newmarket to Newcastle Racecourse (horse finished unplaced), which is around a 480-mile round trip. I only did it once. That was enough. From then on, I let the train take the strain for the more extreme journeys north.

We set off early on the day, and we drove, and drove, and drove. It just goes on and on, and on. The interstate was clear enough, and we cruised along. Outside, the countryside was flat and bleak. The dead earth frozen, the trees skeletal, the tarmac dark. I gazed out of the window at the lifeless scene for hour after hour and was reminded of Cormac McCarthy's novel *The Road*.

I think it was about midway through my fourth lifetime that we reached the racetrack. It had taken five and a half hours, but we were there. I had livened up the last couple hours of the drive cheerfully imagining where I was going to dump the agent's lifeless carcass on the return leg.

The facility was new. It was clean, well managed, and the food was predictable but fine—hot dogs, burgers, fries. The whole facility was fine but predictable. For this was a racetrack newly built only for the casino. There were no hopes, no aspirations, no dreams for this track. It was just a business plan come to life. And the track only existed so that a casino could be built. It was like an unwanted child that comes as a result of wanted sex.

The horses here are numbers to bet on. The jockeys are replaceable unknowns; the trainers are just doing a job. It is strictly business. Jack rode in the allowance, one of the more valuable races on the card, and won it under a polished ride. And it was a good day's work financially, and that's all it was.

So, we got back in the car and headed home, and I decided, after the win, that maybe I should let the agent live after all. But four long hours later, when we were still another two hours from home, I started to imagine him shoulder deep in the dirt, with just his head sticking out, and me, standing there, with a shovel in my hand. (I found out later that the agent had a concealed carry permit. So, it looks like it would have been me who ended up with my head sticking out of the ground. Just shows, doesn't it).

The Mahoning Valley race on January 28 was Jack's fifth win in January, which was okay, but maybe not enough compensation for missing New Year's in Abu Dhabi. However, there were still two more days of racing at Turfway before the end of the month.

On the thirtieth he drew a blank, but he won the first race on the final day of the month and so reached number six. And then he won the seventh race too, which ended the month on seven and another double under his belt. And then he won the eighth. And he was only just beaten a head in the ninth under a storming ride!

And when he came out of the jocks room on a frosty, sparkling-cold Kentucky night for the journey home, all he could do was rue the one that got away.

January total: 8 wins from 86 rides
Bug Year total: 21 wins from 255 rides

Chapter 13

Cheeseburger Soup

istory tells us that all great nations eventually decline. Some, like ancient Rome and Greece are great for many centuries, whilst others may experience a period of greatness that is much briefer. But they all rise from obscurity to prominence, shine for a while, and then fade slowly back into mediocrity.

Whilst not coined as an explanation for the rise and fall of nations, marketing people have a phrase to describe such a phenomenon. It is known as the Product Life Cycle. When shown in graph form, it describes the fairly steep rise in revenue from a new product as it is launched and marketed to the public, until it reaches a plateau, which is when it has reached its mature level of regular income. Here it should roughly stay until a new and better product comes along, at which time the original product shall experience a gradual decline in sales until it eventually disappears from the market. I have heard it said that the product with the longest period of mature sales that still shows no sign of entering decline is Coca-Cola.

Anyway, what is true of cat food seems to be true of great nations. They rise, they shine for a while, and then they decline and fall. Now you can tell where you stand with your cat food by what your sales figures tell you. But a nation is rather more complicated than that. To be sure, the wealth and productivity of a nation is important, but so are its politics, its morals, and the education and welfare of its citizens, as they are the factors that probably decide in which future direction a country is headed. So how do you assess a nation? How can you know where it stands in its life cycle? The answer may surprise you. It is soup.

Soup was the answer to a question that struck me the other day whilst browsing in Kroger supermarket, which we still count as a leisure activity. Its massive size and variety of produce makes us think of it more as a grocery-style theme park than just another store. Anyway, we were wandering the aisles, taking in all the new products on offer and looking for jockey-suitable foodstuffs, when in the soup aisle my eyes browsed past an item, vaguely registered what it said on the tin, and then moved on—before they initiated a skidding handbrake turn and returned their focus, in disbelief, to the words on the tin of soup: *Campbell's Chunky Hearty Cheese-burger*. How? Why? When?

I looked. I thought. And I feared, in that instant, that America may be doomed.

We all know that the United States is famous for fast food, for junk food, for weird combinations. But this was too far, this was literally too much to digest. Who thought of this? What deranged chef thought, *I know what the American people need, a new soup! I shall begin by making a cheeseburger, then I shall cut it up into chunks, and then put it into a pan with a couple of cups of water, and mush it all up.* That is what six-year-olds do when they play at cooking! It is what people who have been out of their heads for three days on crystal meth do, just before they slice off their own tongue and eat that too!

So, I stared at it in disbelief for a while. And you know what? I started to feel guilty. It's irrational I know, as none of this was my fault, and there is nothing I could have done about it had I stayed in America. But I started to imagine myself like some Dennis the Menace–type character, back when I was five, my feet lodged on the outside of the fuselage, my hands clutching my mother's arm, pulling her back, refusing to let her enter the plane.

I felt like a parent who was going away for a while and before leaving told their teenage children to be sure to wash, and clean, and eat properly, and look after each other, and then comes back (admittedly forty-three years later) and finds them still sitting on the couch, still dressed in jeans and still eating junk like teenagers. But they all have grey hair now, and big bellies, and not many teeth. And now it's too late for them. They are going to be slobs forever, and they won't know better than to raise their children as slobs too, and they will be worse than their parents. And that is how I think a country declines. It starts with the soup.

Nearly half a century ago, I left America as a young child. Soup back then, I am sure, would have been chicken noodle, or clam chowder, or tomato, or some other traditional concoction. So here is my theory to measure the state of any nation quickly and simply, to determine whether that nation is rising, coasting along nicely, or in danger of decline. It doesn't have to be soup, it can be any new item really. But the question to ask is this: Does this new product—in this case cheeseburger soup—represent a step forward for our society and its way of life, and how we are perceived by other nations. Are we smarter, healthier, better off, and more appealing in the eyes of others because of this new product. If so, then we are an ambitious nation, still on the rise, and congratulations to Campbell's. Or does this new product just represent a small step forward, a little twist, a small improvement not really needed but appreciated, like heated seats in cars. If that is the case, then that means the people at Campbell's are still conscientious and care about their products and their citizen's perception of them.

Or is this new product lazy, is it tired and cynical, a barely disguised insult to its customers? If so, this means that

Campbell's has lost respect for its fellow citizens, and pride in its product, and instead Wall Street mentality has taken over, and it is chasing every last buck it can get its hands on—and screw you!

And then you know this could be a nation heading toward decline, because Campbell's is producing offensive rubbish, and Americans are eating it. And that wasn't the case forty years ago.

P.S. On the tin it recommends that "for a really hearty meal, just pour over fries." QED.

Chapter 14

The Bug Year: February 2015

Turfway Park

With February came the snow. We had been warned not to spend the winter in Kentucky, to go south to Tampa Bay Downs in Florida, or to Fair Grounds in Louisiana. Not Turfway Park in northern Kentucky, in the middle of the winter, in the middle of the night. But we ignored the warnings.

Kentucky enjoys four well-defined seasons and within them a variable climate. They say if you don't like the weather here, just wait ten minutes. Some winters they get considerable snow and some winters just a dusting. This winter, our first in North America, Kentucky experienced record snowfall and record low temperatures. And we absolutely loved it!

It was magical. The snow fell and blanketed the country-side in thick white duvets, so powdery and dry that you could wade through feet-deep drifts of the stuff and your trousers wouldn't get wet. And when the sky was laser blue, the air you were breathing in felt like it had been triple filtered through arctic glaciers.

In Newmarket, the air is damp in winter and it chills you to the bone, and the wind blows through you, and whips the rain into your face, and howls across the dark heath, and the sun hardly seems to show itself, and life clings on through the darkness, just existing, for months, enduring, fighting on, awaiting the first hint of spring, aching for some relief from the long black winter.

In Kentucky, the sun rises and sets at a civilized hour summer and winter, and when you get a reasonable amount of sunlight hours through the winter then, well, compared to the UK, winter does not feel like a punishment here. In fact, every season here is a new delight. A pleasure, a gift from nature to savour, and enjoy, and relish. At least until race time.

So, the snowy days were fun and a novelty, and our small third floor apartment was cosy and warm, and had a little open fire, so the three of us, plus Geri, would wedge ourselves together onto the tiny (a bit too tiny actually) secondhand couch I had picked up cheaply, and put our feet up, and enjoy a movie. And out of the window you could look across the snow-covered rooves and balconies. And we would enjoy that during the week, as Turfway was only racing weekends now. But come Friday evening, for Jack anyway, it was payback time…

His face would be raw- and purple not red. His fingers and toes devoid of feeling, sometimes his fingers frozen too numb even to change his stick. It was inhumane really, on the worst nights, and I don't know how all the jockeys coped sometimes. But for Jack the winners kept coming.

Will Gracie Shine provided him with a win on the first night's racing, and the following weekend he bagged a double on Friday night and a single win on Saturday, for three individual wins. The next weekend the Saturday card was cancelled due to weather conditions, but he still notched a victory on Sunday afternoon that we all enjoyed, as it was on Elmor, the little bay gelding that had looked after Jack on his very first ride in North America.

The following weekend the boy registered a brace of wins, in spite of the Saturday card being cancelled once again. So, he went into the final weekend of a short month, with only eight days racing thus far, with seven wins to his name. On the Friday card, he landed the second treble of his career (Elmor and Will Gracie Shine bless them, came up trumps again) and had two seconds to go with it. And on the Saturday he bagged another win in the feature allowance race, and was third in the listed John Battaglia Memorial Stakes.

The bug was sizzling hot and challenging for second place for leading rider at the meet. Two nights and one day's work a week (plus a few mornings). Plenty of winners, nice paychecks. It was time for him to buy his first car…

We had been in the States for six months now, and I had been renting a car since day one. When we arrived, I had thought I would buy a modest little secondhand vehicle, but when I realized the mileage we were going to be doing, and when I saw the holes in the roads, and people talking and texting on their phones while doing eighty along the interstate, and the size and the speed of the trucks, and when I researched and found that the death rate on American roads was double that of the UK (I was expecting it to be higher—somewhere around a hundred percent was my guess) I knew some cheap, secondhand run-around was not going to suffice. So, I kept renting, and with all the extra insurance, it bled whatever money we had away. Until, by the time Turfway came around, I not only didn't have money to buy any type of vehicle, I wasn't even sure how long we could keep renting.

But then Jack started winning, and he put money away each week, and by February he had a chunk saved, and it was time for him to buy his first car.

On his days off we started looking around for something suitable for about $10,000 or less.

I was surprised, but you don't seem to get much car here for that money. We were visiting secondhand car dealerships, and they are obviously the same the world over. I wouldn't have trusted the cars, or the car dealers…

It was disappointing, as Jack, like any young lad, was really excited about getting his first car. And I was worried because I knew we had to get something, but everything we saw was, even to my untrained eye, a heap of junk.

After a week or so we were returning from another fruitless journey to view a large piece of rust that someone wanted about eight thousand for when we passed a Mercedes dealership, and, on a whim, I pulled in. I knew it was doubtful that they would have anything in our price range, but maybe someone might have traded something in, and it might be an older Mercedes, and at least this was an authorized dealership.

We were greeted by a genial gentleman by the name of Larry Cartwright. I don't recall how I was dressed that day, but I am normally fairly hairy at that time of year, and I doubt I looked very much like a promising Mercedes customer, I probably looked more like someone who could use a bit of spare change.

But Larry doesn't judge a book by its cover. He extended Jack and I every courtesy, and as soon as he found out Jack's profession he took even greater interest, being an avid race fan himself.

We soon established that there was nothing in the dealership that we could afford without financing, and we had already discovered the catch with credit since we arrived in the country. Without a credit history, you couldn't get any. So, we found ourselves in a chicken and egg scenario and had already been turned down for several minor forms of credit we had applied for—for no reason other than to start getting a credit history. I therefore had absolutely no hope that we could obtain financing to buy a Mercedes, when we had failed to secure any to purchase a pair of jeans.

Larry, however, seemed oblivious to our status and started showing us cars from their pre-approved used range, inviting Jack and I to test drive two or three C-classes. And they were great. And after driving basic hire cars for six months, it was like stepping off of a tractor and into a spaceship. Superior lovely cars, but they cost the best part of $20k more than we had.

And then Larry suggested maybe we were aiming a little too low with the C-class. "You get so much more with an E-class," he told us. So, we tested a couple of them. And he was right! And so we wasted more of Larry's time—and the third E-class we tried was beautiful. A black E 350, six years old, only forty thousand miles on the clock, luxury AMG body kit, tinted windows, top of the range sound system, full leather interior, voice activated navigation and stereo system, Mercedes emergency twenty-four-hour assistance. And it drove better than it looked. Jack and I were in love. But we may as well have been pining over Taylor Swift for all the chance we had. It was a steal at $25,000. But we would have to steal $17,000 to get it.

Undeterred by our semi-refugee status, Larry told us to bring in all the documentation we had the next day, and we sat down with him and their finance manager, who at least kindly went through the motions with us, instead of just saying sorry and kicking us out of the office as I was expecting. I don't know how long I thought the charade would go on, but I was finding it hard to maintain the pretence, knowing how disappointed Jack was going to be.

It was sometime later that evening when Larry rang me. All he said was "congratulations." And I thought, *Damn, this really is a great country!* And I meant it, and I'll tell you why. It's because when we wanted that Mercedes, people tried to help us get it; they went out of their way to help us get it. And yes, there was something in it for them, but there was something in it for us too. Mercedes was happy, Larry was happy, and Jack was ecstatic!

So, Vicky got a bit of a surprise when we picked her up from work the next day. And when all the excitement had died down, we decided, sensibly in my opinion, that we ought to see about getting Jack a driver's licence.

He still has the car, and it's all paid off, and he loves it. In fact, as I am writing this—and this is the truth—he is outside right now, washing it.

We drove a total of seventy-two thousand miles during Jack's bug year. That's nearly three times around the circumference of the Earth. And on those many long journeys, after many a disappointing day at the races, that car was our saving grace, our pleasure, our reliable friend. Like Larry.

February total: 11 wins from 60 rides
Bug Year total: 32 wins from 315 rides

Chapter 15

The Bug Year: March 2015

Turfway Park

The bug rolled into Turfway Park, in his Mercedes, on the first of March and raced into the winner's enclosure on his first mount of the night, then finished fourth, then second on his next two, and then won on his final two rides. He was flying now and making the most of every opportunity sent his way.

Vicky and I were enjoying going racing with him in the evenings and watching his success. It is very difficult watching your nearest and dearest race, but he was doing what he had dreamed of since he was a tiny boy.

Whenever anyone had asked him what he was going to be when he grew up, he would say he was going to be a jockey.

And whilst for many youngsters it might be a pipe dream to become a professional sportsman (it was for me), for Jack, born and raised in the sport, it just seemed to him the most natural thing in the world to do.

But even for those youngsters born into the sport, few have the necessary skill, dedication, balance, athleticism, and nerve to convert their childish dreams into reality.

The first thing Jack saw when introduced to the wider world for the first time by his nervous new mother were racehorses' heads peering over stable doors at him in his pram. The horse and the baby human both bemused, each wondering at the other, each gentle and innocent by nature, but one with the size and strength of a god, the other helpless and small, but with eyes that could learn and perceive.

He had a quiet gentle way about him Jack, he still has, and animals like that and bond with him quickly. Our stable star, Rushcutter Bay, a topflight sprinter with a temperament worse than his trainer's, would lower his head for Jack in his toddler years and let him poke and stroke him, his large brown eyes taking him in, his ears pricked with interest. I could have let Jack sleep in the stable with that horse, a horse who seemed to spend the rest of his waking hours devising ways to despatch me, and as many of my staff as possible, into the afterlife.

He was the first horse Jack ever sat on. A graded-stakes winning racehorse, who would buck and spin and resent every moment I was on his back. But who would walk carefully around the yard like a riding school pony when I put Jack on him.

At the age of five, Jack got his own pony, a little shit by the name of Oscar. Knee high to a cricket and totally oblivious to the welfare of the little kid upon his back. He was interested only in putting as much food in his belly as he could, and like many small ponies, he was willful and spoilt, and between us we could hardly manage this little Thelwell caricature come to life.

The pony scared Jack a bit, and he stopped riding for a few years until, at about the age of ten, he asked if he could start again. So we took him for lessons at the local riding school, and there the nervous little boy who asked to be led into and out of the riding arena pushed himself to master the rising trot, and canter, and jumping little poles.

At age eleven, we got him another little pony called Sweet Pea; she was fine, but nappy, and always wanted to call it a day and head home when ridden out. But Jack was older now, and one day, when she was refusing to go where he wanted, he kicked his legs out of the stirrup irons, growled at her, and with his legs locked on her sides and his arms shaking the reins, he drilled her forward, and by sheer force of will he made her submit to him. And a horseman was born.

By thirteen, he was exercising our racehorses out on Newmarket Heath before school. The small boy getting attention from the other strings as they rode by and, even at that time, compliments for how he rode. There would be cheers of encouragement from the lads when he would sit a buck or a spin, leaving him white faced but proud.

He started pony racing at this time. The pony we secured for him was an undersize Thoroughbred, as were most of the entries in these contests, so it was a taste of the real thing. She went by the name of Gwen, and she was without doubt the ugliest, most sour, and wicked creature I have ever encountered. She was ferociously vicious with her teeth, and the evil faces she pulled when tacking her up would have given a serial killer nightmares.

She would regularly throw Jack in the most deliberate and nasty ways and take off loose across the heath. But if you took her hunting or racing, she was as workmanlike, tough, and honest as you could ask.

His first race was at Stratford Racecourse in Stratford-upon-Avon. He was fourteen the first time he donned the silks for a race. He hadn't eaten the whole day, was white as a sheet, and started dry retching about two hours before his ride.

I drank a beer and when the time came, threw him up on the pony in the paddock. No sooner was he on than it jinked at another pony misbehaving and dropped him. So, I legged him up again, and he was off, even whiter than before. I really didn't think, with all the nervous energy he had expended and the lack of food, that he would have the strength to ride the mare to the start, much less in a race. But he got there okay. And, as we waited for the contest, even through the beer, I was nervous. And now Vicky was as white as Jack!

After about three false starts caused by recalcitrant ponies and unshipped riders, they were off. Jack's mare lacked early speed and was trailing the field, but he started to pass a couple as they entered the home turn. I didn't expect much more and couldn't see too well, but then a pony appeared up the rail, its rider a whirling dervish of activity, drilling and pumping for all he was worth, and they flew past several runners to get up late for third place.

He came back with eyes blazing and told me about what had happened during every furlong of the race, about how she travelled, and which parts of the race went right, and which parts were wrong for her. And I thought: *Fuck me.*

He ended up winning the East Anglian pony racing championship final at Fakenham Racecourse in Norfolk. It was a great day. Vicky and I were so pleased for him, he wasn't a child who won at school sports day, or who was bigger or stronger or louder than the other boys. So this was his moment to shine and a very just reward for pushing himself to do it, in spite of all his nerves.

Not long after, he enrolled at the British Racing School to take their two-year course for youngsters intending to enter the racing industry. It involved taking a day out of school each week, which was a concern, as he comes from a family which has many highflying academic achievers, and it was obvious his school results would suffer. But as he repeatedly told his mother and father when the subject of exams came up, "What do I need them for? I'm going to be a jockey."

It was the British Racing School that coordinated with the North American Racing Academy (NARA) to arrange for Jack and his best friend and fellow student Ben Rabillard, to come on an exchange visit to Lexington, where NARA's founders, legendary ex-rider Chris McCarron, and Remi Bellocq, showed them such a good time that it inspired in him a desire to come back one day as a jockey and race ride in America.

And he did. And here he was now into the last month of the Turfway Park meet, and he had just ridden seven winners in three days.

A treble on the first day of the month had got him off to a flier. The first full weekend yielded one win, but the following weekend he bagged three more victories, so he went into the next week with seven wins under his belt from just seven days racing. For Jack this was to be his last weekend of the Turfway meet as he had picked up a minor riding suspension that ruled him out of the last few days. So, he was hoping to end the meeting as he'd started it—with winners.

It was not to be, however. The final weekend he rode, he drew a blank. So now his tack was to head back down to Keeneland with his valet for their prestigious spring meet. No more late nights, no more travelling for a month. Turfway had been great, but now the big meets were around the corner, and he was keen to go there and bag that dreamed of first victory at his local and feted track without further delay!

March total: 7 wins from 50 rides
Bug Year total: 39 wins from 365 rides

Chapter 16

The Bug Year: April 2015

Keeneland, Indiana Grand

Our first experience of Keeneland had been in the autumn, when it is regal. Dressed in its reds and golds and rusts and pinks and bronzes. But in the spring, it is a delightful feast of white and pink blossom, making the place delicate and pretty. And the girls arrive for the races in their spring dresses, and the boys in their jackets and bow ties, and the place is as fine a place to be on a perfect sunny day, as mere humans can contrive to deliver. In fact, sometimes Keeneland seems almost surreal in its perfection; it is so tidy, so manicured, so perfect, sometimes it seems more like someone's daydream of a perfect day's racing than a reality.

And, indeed, it was a shame that reality did have to intrude. But it did. And it came as a bucket of cold water over us. And the message was, "Turfway doesn't count for anything here. And bugs count for even less."

It wasn't that he didn't get mounts, he did, though not many. It was just that he didn't get offered any that had any real shot of winning. We had thought that his success at Turfway might count for something. That now that he had shown he could win, maybe one or two of the bigger Kentucky outfits would give Jack a shot. But they didn't. The wall was still up, and I couldn't understand why. He rode well, he was stylish, and was value for his weight allowance. But I am his dad, and when I look back now, although I still think he rode well and probably deserved some better mounts than he received, I see that trying to make the light weights his claim dictated left him weak in a finish.

More importantly, probably, we were not approaching his bug year the way it is traditionally done in the States. Jack should probably have been at a small track somewhere, continuing to ride away on live mounts, riding more winners in small races, as he had been doing all winter. That is how it mostly happens here if a bug wants to ride a lot of winners in their short twelve-month apprenticeship. So as usual, I was steering Jack seemingly down a losing path, getting it all wrong again. But this time there was at least some method to my madness.

And it was this. When Jack was riding at Keeneland, he was competing against a concentrated band of jockeys as good as you will find anywhere in the world at one racetrack on one day. He could observe them in the weighing room and listen to them, and they were generous with their time with him. He received advice personally from some of the elite athletes in his sport, people at the top of their games. And on the track when he was competing against them, they would ride correctly but competitively against him. They might keep him tight on the rail or close the gap if he unwisely tried to go up their inner. They showed him the importance of saving ground, of getting a horse to change leads at the correct times, of staying in on the turn.

He saw and learned many things, and nearly all of it was positive, and useful, and traits and habits of people who had succeeded. He saw and learned how successful people are, and he saw their attitudes, and he got their advice—and he wasn't going to get that off his old man.

So, I am not saying that there are no good riders at the small tracks, because there are, some very good ones, but I wanted him to learn, to see how sometimes even a lesser rider can raise his game and have business at the highest level, and that sometimes a very talented rider can end up riding the minor tracks. To see that riding ability is just one determinant of how a jockey ends up winning at Keeneland. That how they are as people, how they conduct themselves, and how they believe in themselves and value themselves matters. I wanted him to see that, to be around those people, because he had grown up watching his parents struggle, and I didn't want him to think that was how it had to be for him. And I think, after listening to Jack recount some tales of the jocks room that—with one or two hair-raising exceptions!—I was right.

But none of that stopped the wheels falling off the bus once more. The winners had stopped again. And the bug boy's career spluttered and stalled, and crawled along all month.

There was one highlight though. He got to ride in the Giant's Causeway Stakes at Keeneland. A stakes race is a big deal in horse racing; a stakes race at Keeneland is a very big deal. The mare was an outsider, but it was still good of her connections to entrust the mount to an apprentice as they cannot claim their weight allowance in stakes races. So he would be going head-to-head with the top jockeys at level weights in a stakes race at Keeneland in the spring—there are worse things to do than that you know.

It was a lovely sunny spring day, and the people basked in the sun and drank their cocktails and laughed and smiled. And the paddocks were green, and the horses were shiny and brown, and the jockeys' colours dazzled in the sun. And Jack Gilligan came into the paddock, a shamrock on his silks.

Javier Castellano, North America's champion jockey was in the paddock, as was Corey Lanerie, the leading rider on the Kentucky circuit; Joel Rosario, top go-to New York–based rider; Florent "Frenchie" Geroux, up-and-coming star, winning stakes races at a higher rate than any other rider in the country. Top riders, top men, doing a tough job well, and the kid, in amongst them. A fish trying to swim with the sharks.

They were out of the gate like a flash, and he was up in his irons and perched easily on the mare as she raced on the outer in second. Five and a half furlongs on turf, one sharp left-hand turn followed by a two-furlong homestretch. She moved to the lead on the bend, and when they straightened up for home, he shook the reins at the 50/1 shot, and she opened up, she stretched and set sail for home, and with a furlong to run, with the crowd cheering, she was still in the lead, and for a few seconds, it looked like they could pull a mighty upset. But then she got tired, and her stride shortened slightly, and the favourites caught her. And Frenchie picked up another Stakes. But she had run her heart out for sixth, the best performance of her career to date. And it gave Jack a taste of the big time, of what could maybe lay ahead, for him, someday. And he liked it.

April total: 0 wins from 31 rides
Bug Year total: 39 wins from 396 rides

Chapter 17

The Derby

In the end, it all comes down to this. *All the Pretty Horses,* all the racetracks, all the breeding farms, all the stallions, all the mares, all the yearlings, all the foals, all the auctions, all the trainers, all the grooms, all the hotwalkers, all the exercise riders, all the forage merchants, all the feed men, all the saddlers, all the farriers, all the vets. All the jockeys. In the end, all of it. All of them. Is about the greatest two minutes in sport.

When the best three-year-old in the nation flashes past that winning post in front (so long as it is a colt), it instantly becomes the most valuable Thoroughbred racehorse in North America. Five million dollars for a lesser one, twenty million plus for a great one. That is what they are suddenly worth.

And this is a market value, a hard-headed assessment of risk versus rewards. You see, when that three-year-old retires to stud later that year or the next, it will be in demand to cover a hundred or more mares a year. His stud fee will be at least $20,000 a cover, maybe many multiples of that. And then, if his progeny themselves show talent and become champions, his fee will go up again. Stallion fees in North America have reached $500,000 per cover. Multiply that by a hundred mares a year. Then multiply that by up to twenty years of service. More money is at stake than a layman could ever have guessed.

Federico Tesio, legendary Italian Thoroughbred breeder of the last century said,

"The Thoroughbred exists because its selection has depended, not on experts, technicians, or zoologists, but on a piece of wood: the winning post of the Epsom Derby. If you base your criteria on anything else, you will get something else, not the Thoroughbred."

And just as the most feted new sire in Europe each year is the winner of the Epsom Derby, the most feted new stallion each year in North America is the winner of the Kentucky Derby, because that is the horse who, under the most demanding conditions, in the biggest field, against the best horses, over a further distance, emerged victorious. It won the purest test, to produce the purest champion. Or at least it was until race day medications were allowed.

I won't go into that topic here, except to say that the purpose of horse racing, the raison d'etre of it all, was originally for two gentlemen to pit their swiftest, soundest, best horses against each other to determine the best. And the best was bred to the best to improve the breed. If the horse bled or couldn't stay sound, it would not win, and it would not be bred from, because it was found to be not fit for purpose. And now, with medication, horses not as intrinsically fit for purpose are sometimes beating sounder specimens and taking place in front of them at stud, passing on their faulty genes to future generations.

A horse bleeding or going lame is not a fault requiring fixing in horse racing. It is natural selection, and a consequence of pitting horses against each other in competition. To identify the swiftest, the soundest, the most suitable. The fittest.

I have been to quite a few Epsom Derbies. I lived in and around Epsom for many years as a youngster, and I was a young boy when I went the first time. You had never seen anything like it back then. Some say a quarter of a million people went, some say it was more like a half million. I don't know. But I know that when I was young, so many people went that from the infield, in the cheap seats, the free seats, on the downs, amongst the working men, the travellers, the vagabonds and the pickpockets, you would probably fail to see even a glimpse of a horse the whole day, sometimes it took time to find out who had even won the big event. Most years I would only catch a glimpse of colourful jockeys' hats moving smoothly together at speed, over the heads of the multitudes in front of me.

It was a different thing then, going to the derby. Still owing more to the Victorian age than the modern one. When the original Londoners, the working Londoners, still lived in the capital. That one day of the year, they would get on the trains and head to Epsom, and come out, and see some grass, and breathe some fresh air, and gaze on the city whence they had come, just visible from the Downs, and bring their energy, and their voices, and their unself-conscious banter, before returning, a bit ruffled and happy, back to the great city. It was an ancient thing, cockled eels and whelks for sale. The fair, the gypsies, find the lady, watch your wallet, beer. No champagne. Not here. Not out on the downs, where the real derby was going on.

I loved being in amongst it, just being part of this great gathering of humanity, of people lying on the grass, talking, drinking, jeering, cheering, laughing, betting, shouting. Smoking their cigarettes. Working men enjoying a day off, a day out. Not much money to spend, not much money needed. Just enough for tobacco, a few beers, a few bets, a cheap news-paper folded up with the runners and riders. God provided the rest. Well, God and the nobility, the millionaires, the princes racing their horses. Two different worlds touching, just a strip of grass dividing them. A strip of grass—and a world. But all, for different reasons, cheering those colts with those colourful riders home on that beautiful turf. Summer in England.

And now it was spring in Kentucky. And here I was again, walking to a racetrack, something I hadn't done in years, our car abandoned to parking a mile away from the course. A

116

milling throng walking in one direction, with one intention, to go have some fun, to go see a derby.

It is more colourful here in Kentucky. Men don't wear jackets like these in the UK; I didn't wear jackets like these in the UK. I did here. I joined in. You have to join in, otherwise what is the point? Mad clothes for a mad day. A day of madness. The brightest coloured mob you will ever see, all paths leading to Churchill Downs. One hundred and seventy thousand spectators the year I went. The year American Pharoah won. I picked a good year.

You can buy seats at the Kentucky Derby. There are seventy thousand of them. You should buy a seat, I suppose; they run from a hundred dollars up to thousands each. But we only decided last minute, and I was too cheap, and that's not how I do a derby.

So we stood all day, stood and watched, by the paddock mostly, drank beers out of a can, had some bets, a hot dog ruined my jacket. And we talked, and laughed, and watched all the people. Crazy guys with loud checked jackets, bow ties, and mad hats. Girls in crazy outfits, models in haute couture. Rich people, poor people. The horses don't know. They don't know what they are worth. American Pharoah didn't know all these people came, all these people travelled, all these people planned and saved to come and see him. That all these people were excited to see him.

I was excited to see him. I wanted to be by the paddock. I can see him walk by me now. I have forgotten the pretty girls, but I remember that horse. I had wanted to see him, had seen his trials on television and thought he was special, there was something about him, his stride, his demeanour.

He wasn't anything special to look at though. He wasn't a poser, wasn't flashy. Workmanlike, unfussy. A good eye. They always have a good eye, the best ones. The head and the eye. You can see, as you can with people, if you look. If you don't let them deceive you with words.

Well, horses can't talk. Trainers wouldn't like horses that talked. Spilling the beans to the owners, or the jockey, or the bettors. Trainers wouldn't like that one little bit.

Horses don't talk; they work. They have always worked for man, for nothing but a bit of food, a bit of care. They have worked for us for millennia, and we have domesticated them, and bred them for our purposes, and used them for the strength that they have, that we lack. And they helped us build civilizations and fight wars and, with two steps forward then one step back, to progress. They helped us so well that they found themselves not needed any longer. Victims to progress. Unemployed. Destined for extinction.

But we found we loved them. We found we missed them. Our giant friends. Man's truest friend. So, we took them as companions, for our pleasure. We bred them to enjoy, to ride, to spend our leisure time with, and some, to race. And suddenly there were more horses than there had ever been before.

We got out to the front for the race. I listened to the crowd sing "My Old Kentucky Home," a venerable tradition, an American thing. A show thing. It was moving, standing there, surrounded, everybody ready now, everyone ready for the contest, the showdown. The Run for the Roses.

It is a roar not a race, an outpouring, a moment in time. Too many horses, most covered in dirt, becoming anonymous, difficult to pick out. American Pharoah was easy to see, though, his bright turquoise and gold colours clean, up in front, out wide, avoiding the mud. But up front and out wide is the long way, the hard way. You have to be superior to win like that over that distance.

He was superior. And he returned to his blanket of red roses, with the stands ablaze with noise and colour. The right result, that always helps. We always like the right result, don't we? He even had the right name, in a way.

And that was it. The show was over. The day was done. It was time to fight our way out, amongst the drunk, the lame, the loud, the tired, the weary. But we had done it. We had been there. The year American Pharoah won. A piece of history, and we were there. Just us and 170,000 of our closest friends.

And that is the thing about the derby. Each one is a piece of history. Each one is in the newspapers, reported all over the world, in the media. Each one is an event recorded by humanity. And you can be there, experience it, be part of it, for a few dollars—or a few million. Your choice. And one way or the other, you can say you were there. And you will remember it forever.

Chapter 18

The Bug Year: May 2015

Churchill Downs, Indiana Grand, Belterra Park

They say spring comes in like a lion and goes out like a lamb. Well, so it was with Jack's bug year. He had come out of Turfway Park's winter meet roaring through the nights, with winners and places aplenty. But now, at the beginning of May, with summer around the corner, it had been seven long weeks since his last winner.

At least when winner number forty came it was at the most famous racetrack in North America. Churchill Downs, the home of the Kentucky Derby. And he rode his winner at the track just five days after eighteen three-year-old colts thundered down the very same patch of dirt, competing for victory in the one hundred and forty first consecutive running of the event.

It was quieter, of course, than Derby week, when every day crowds are huge, and clothes are fine, or loud, or both. But it was still much busier than the rest of the year, there was still a buzz. It was like a wedding after the bride and groom had left, but the band was still playing a bit, and the bar was still open, and the youngsters were not ready to stop partying just yet.

After the win, after he pulled up around the backstretch, after he yanked his dirty goggles down, after he turned the tired filly around, Jack set off back, cantering quietly, standing up and relaxed on her now, heading toward the winner's enclosure near the winning post. And as he came back down the stretch, in front of the stands, the crowd greeted the victor with a little roar, and Jack could hear them cheering, for him and the filly, and he told me later he looked up at the grandstand—and it is huge—and he said he could see splashes of colour dotted everywhere from the people's clothes, all over the massive stands.

So, it was just one win, but it was one to savour. And he had now ridden winners at grade one tracks—the biggest, on two continents.

May was good overall, away from the racetrack. Ben, Jack's best friend from back home in England, was over for a holiday with his father, Olivier, and they stayed with us. The pool was open at the apartment, Lexington was sunny and beautiful, we went to the Kentucky Derby, drank wine on the balcony at night, and the two boys went off in the car exploring Lexington, going to the mall, to the movies, hoping to meet girls, being teenagers, having fun.

But for Jack the work continued in between. May brought better runners, more places, and two more winners, both at Indiana. One of them a nice maiden winner in a $32,000 race. But it was much less than hoped for, much less than needed to consider his bug year a success, to judge the gamble of coming here as having been worthwhile.

Chris McCarron had told us that if you can't ride much more than forty winners in your bug year, you need to think about taking up another job. And it was the end of May now, and he had only just passed forty wins after eight months of his bug, and he'd only ridden three winners over the past two months, and there was no reason to suppose things would be getting significantly better any time soon.

I was struggling really. I knew only too well from my own career how much it hurt to be willing and capable but not called, not wanted, not needed, to be dismissed. It was silly of course. I was placing my experiences on his shoulders. He was fine, and he was doing great by every ordinary metric of a youngster's life. He had a green card allowing him to work and live in the richest country on Earth and was a British citizen, born in one of the most historically important countries in the world. And with that citizenship he was also free to travel, live, and work, if he so desired, throughout Europe (for now at least). For those things alone he was blessed compared to most citizens of the world. And he was making good money doing the job he had dreamed about. So what if he had a couple of quiet months? In the great scheme of things, it didn't matter at all of course.

And I can see now that he wasn't ready then, that it was for the best that his ascent was coming in fits and starts, giving him a chance to pause for breath now and then, to acclimatize on his way up.

The fastest, most direct route to the top of the mountain is the steepest, the toughest, and the most precarious. And if or when that summit is reached, what then? You can try to stay there as long as you can, but eventually you have to start your descent—because from the summit there is nowhere else to go.

The slower, more leisurely climb up the mountain affords time to enjoy the journey itself, to take in the views and appreciate them, to stand and breathe in the air and enjoy where you are, how high you have climbed. And one day you may even look to the top, to the people clinging on to the tip, and think, *You know what, the view from where I am right now looks pretty good to me.*

But, like I said, that is my considered philosophy now. Not then. Back then I was going nuts.

May total: 3 wins from 37 rides
Bug Year total: 42 wins from 433 rides

Chapter 19

The Twin Spires

I don't know how many of you are familiar with the television series *The Walking Dead*, a show that follows the fortunes of a desperate group of survivors who find themselves living in a nightmare zombie apocalypse. But it's just that the last half mile on the approach to Churchill Downs sometimes feels like you have inadvertently taken a wrong turn and found yourself driving through a live set of the show. I have never seen so many obviously troubled people in such a small area in my life. Poor, semi-homeless, disturbed. Disturbing. It is sometimes frightening, sometimes blackly comical, and always quite sad.

On busy days, many of the houses nearest the track turn their front yards into unofficial car parks, and some of the saner locals hold pieces of cardboard advertising parking for five or ten dollars, hoping to attract three or four cars each. You have to be pretty poor to spend a day doing that.

There was one guy who, for a whole season, stood by the side of the road with his cardboard sign and became a bit of a hero to Jack and myself. This man would target me each day as I began to filter left into the Churchill car park where Jack had accreditation for the jockeys' parking. He was implacable and completely undeterred by the badge dangling from our rearview mirror. He would signal my car his way as assuredly as any aircraft marshal, his booming, confident voice tempting me, like a large, hairy, scruffily dressed siren, toward the rocks of five-dollar parking on, quite decidedly, the wrong side of the street.

This man was so determined in his quest to park me, that when I looked in my rearview mirror as I passed him, I would be startled to find him still signalling to me, still convinced he could close the deal, even as I was disappearing into the distance, and we would hear him calling to us even as we crossed the oncoming traffic and drove into Churchill Downs.

If I had a Wall Street brokerage, or even a decent car dealership, I would have hired that guy. We don't see him there anymore, and I really do hope that someday I will come across him at Churchill, in an expensive suit, with an expensive watch, gold rings on his fingers, and a trophy woman by his side, because in another life that's who he could have been. And in

America, sometimes, you feel there really is a chance, even if just a very small one, that it could just happen for him yet.

After the drive into the track, the great white fortress-like appearance of the place makes sense. When you step through the entrance, it feels like you have entered a sanctuary. Huge walls and wire fences keeping the scary things out. This is not an unusual situation in America, even if the wall isn't always physical.

Churchill Downs racetrack was the idea of Colonel Meriwether Lewis Clark, who was inspired to create a showcase race in the state after a visit to Europe where he attended the Epsom Derby. He leased some land from his uncles, John and Henry Churchill, and the inaugural running of the Kentucky Derby was held in 1875, ninety-five years after the first running of the original at Epsom. The winner was the three-year-old colt Aristides, ridden by Oliver Lewis and trained by Ansel Williamson, both of whom were African Americans. Lewis was born a free man, but Williamson was born a slave, and slavery had only been abolished for ten years, when he placed himself in the history books forever. The "Run for the Roses" has taken place, uninterrupted, every year since, and the Kentucky Derby is now the longest consecutively run sporting event in the United States.

Churchill Downs, like Epsom Downs, is synonymous with its biggest race. And like Epsom, to a large extent it exists for its greatest race. Whilst Epsom Downs hosts only a handful of race days outside of its big week, Churchill Downs races up to five days a week, four months of the year. And that can create a bit of a problem, when a facility built to cater to a crowd of one hundred and seventy thousand people hosts race days with a crowd of around five thousand. I do like Churchill Downs, high quality horses, top jockeys and trainers, and well-maintained tracks. But it is a cavernous place, so on a regular race day, it can lack atmosphere.

That first week of May though—Derby week—it is not only the track that is bustling and lit up, the whole city of Louisville is. There are parties, activities, fireworks, music, food and drink. It is a week-long festival, racing by day and socializing by night, and the city embraces it.

During the July festival in Newmarket, if you drove down the high street at night, you might see more takeaway food wrappers than usual discarded in the street, more blood and vomit, perhaps, than is usual on an average night. But you would not see festivities, families milling around, couples together, people laughing and enjoying themselves and behaving themselves, and novelties and entertainments and distractions for all.

In England, a big sporting event is often seen as an occasion for a very large number of attendees (myself sometimes amongst them) to embark on a Viking style nihilistic orgy of drinking, perhaps culminating in sex for the lucky few, brawling for the rejected, and doner kebabs for the also-rans. People in America embrace sporting events, but generally in a more relaxed way, they are not as keyed up, as aggressive, as intense. People drink plenty but seem to pace themselves; they eat well and enjoy the occasion. The atmosphere is not as ferocious over here for most race days. Sometimes I miss that. Mostly I don't.

Jack's first few rides at Churchill were nothing to note, trailing around the back on outsiders. But the first time he walked down the steps from the jocks room into the paddock alongside the likes of three-time Kentucky Derby winning jockey Calvin Borel, and Robby Albarado, and other top American riders, it felt like something special. These are some of the elite riders in North America, and to compete against them is both a privilege and a challenge.

It may seem simple riding the American tracks, one mile, left-hand level oval. All the same—more or less. Left hand down and away you go. But the uniformity and short straights mean small advantages are important to take. In Europe, you might have a half-mile home straight and being slightly wide on the turn, or slightly out of your ground probably does not end your chances; the field turns into the straight, and the race builds to a crescendo and most horses get their chance.

In the USA races are run at a ferocious early pace, with a two furlong turn at the business end of the race, and a less than two furlong straight. If you are swung wide on the turn or find yourself further back than you should be, especially with the dirt kicking up into the horse's face, then your chance is probably gone. So, when every single one of your fellow jockeys has ridden not hundreds, but thousands of winners around these tracks, they all know, depending on the race distance, their draw, the track conditions, and their horse's preferences, exactly where they want to be at every stage of the race. And they know how to get there.

So as an inexperienced apprentice, you are regularly going to find yourself put into bad spots if you don't learn quickly what you have to do, and when.

So, there was a learning curve for Jack, which was the point of the whole venture anyway.

The week after the derby, he was booked to ride La Jolla D'oro, a nice three-year-old filly who had provided Jack with one of his four wins on the first weekend of the Turfway Park meet the previous December. She was his self-pronounced favourite regular mount to date in the USA—even if he was a bit scared of her senior trainer, ex-jockey, gruff-talking, but good-hearted Ernie Retamoza.

It was Thursday the sixth of May, and it was nice to have Ben and Olivier with us on a warm, sunny evening at Churchill Downs. Jack and Ben had grown up together in Newmarket, had raced each other around the heath dressed up as jockeys as kids, watched the movie *Seabiscuit* a hundred times, and talked excitedly about when they would be jockeys. They both competed in pony racing together, and now Jack was up in the jocks room amongst the senior riders, no doubt learning things he never learned at school.

In spite of Ernie telling Jack—and nearly everyone else he encountered—that they were "gonna get the money," it seemed no one was listening as the filly was the outsider of the field at 25/1. *This isn't Turfway Park,* the bettors seemed to be saying.

When I saw her in the paddock, she looked well, a neat, pretty, dark bay filly. I thought she stood up nicely against her competitors. Jack came into the paddock with the other jockeys, and no doubt Ernie told him again how the money was as good as in the bank.

She broke well in the race and was one of three disputing second place early. Jack in his red silks was perched quietly behind the dark filly's mane. As they entered the home turn, the pace started to increase, and the field tightened up on each other. Halfway around the bend, La Jolla couldn't hold her position as two challenged on the outer. They squeezed down on her, and Jack had to pull back out of the melee. With a length lost he switched her out; she was in fourth now as the field turned for home. She swung into the homestretch on the outer but now had a clear run down the straight, and with no dirt being kicked in her face, she began to lengthen under Jack's urgings. And as Ben and Olivier and I shouted Jack down the stretch, they came by us to take the lead. *A study in scarlet,* heading for victory, passing the wire in front, under the twin spires, basked in the warm Kentucky sun, on a spring evening.

We flung our programs in the air, and we hugged each other like we had just won The Roses, not an $8,000 claimer. And old, bowlegged Ernie was there to greet Jack as he came back into the winner's enclosure. And I thought he nearly let a smile crack his face. Because he was right. They did get the money!

Chapter 20

The Triple Crown. Part One. The Kentucky Derby

I didn't know it at the time, of course. But when I stood beside him at Churchill Downs that morning, I was looking at the horse who would go on to become the first American Triple Crown winner in thirty-seven years.

He stood quietly, waiting at the entrance to the track, waiting his turn to do his morning work. He didn't look special. He looked average, a plain bay, no flashes of white, just a nut-brown coat and a black mane and tail. He was average height for a racehorse, average build, an ok head. He wasn't prancing or snorting; he wasn't surrounded by an entourage, just him and his rider, with his groom at his shoulder, all of them relaxed, slouching slightly, waiting their turn. This was the horse who had just won the Kentucky Derby, standing there, like Rocinante resting from the Spanish sun.

There was only one sign he was special. It was when you looked toward the track. It was when you began to realize that all the other horses, all the other hundreds and hundreds of equine athletes that needed to exercise that morning, were vacating the track. And then the track was harrowed. And then, when it was empty, and silent, and pristine, that was when American Pharoah went out, with the track to himself, to exercise. And then there was nothing ordinary or average about him at all.

It is his stride that marks him out. He has the stride of a bigger horse, the stride of a longer, more powerful horse. He moves like gravity presses down less on him than others. His stride is fluent and perfect and powerful and long. And it doesn't falter, it doesn't weaken, it doesn't yield. Even when his mile gallop was over, the stride kept propelling him along while his rider struggled to ease him down.

There is a period of suspension when a horse gallops. A period when all four legs are off the ground simultaneously, when the horse is just gliding forward through the air, legs tucked beneath him. American Pharoah seemed to spend longer in this phase than other horses. You don't have to be an expert when you watch American Pharoah gallop to know he is good.

I was at the derby. It was ferocious. The huge grandstand under the twin spires seats seventy thousand people, an unbelievable number for a racetrack. And that left another hundred thousand standing.

It is a long day. The first race goes off before noon, but the derby itself isn't run until nearly seven in the evening. It is nearly two hours from the race before the derby until the event itself. But time doesn't drag, there is always something to catch your eye, some moment to get caught up in. The horses, the races, the noise, the people, the clothes, the hats. Shouting, cheering, laughter, talking, posing, eating, drinking too much, spending too much, getting lost in the moment. Escaping for a while. For a day.

Eventually it was time. The horses entered the paddock. This was the first time I had ever seen him in the flesh. The horse who was destined for greatness, marked out. The chosen one. The special one. He didn't prance or dance, he knew what his job was, he knew what was to come; he was to do what he'd been bred for, and I could see in his eye he was ready.

From an initial debut defeat at Del Mar the previous summer, he had racked up four consecutive wins, three of them grade one events, as high as you can go. But this was the Kentucky Derby. The big one. The greatest two minutes in sport.

Field sizes on the dirt in America seldom get close to their maximum of twelve runners, and races rarely exceed a mile in length. The derby this year had eighteen runners due to go to post and would be run over a distance of a mile and a quarter.

For those familiar with the Epsom Derby, you might say, *So what?* After all, that event has large fields and is run over a mile and a half. But dirt racing is not like turf racing. Not one little bit. There is no conservation of energy on dirt, no bounce, no springing off the lush sward. Dirt is dirt, it lays there soft on top until they hit the hard clay base beneath. No spring, no bounce, stamina sapping, leg weakening, jarring, hard, unforgiving, uncaring, brutal, tough. And it sprays up from the horses' hooves, kicking into the faces of the runners and riders behind, stinging them, blinding them, discouraging them, disheartening them, beating them. And all the while one hundred and seventy thousand people look on, roaring, their faces red, their fists clenched, primitive, uncivilized, aggressive. The biggest mob on Earth, lost in each blurring moment.

And then he won. He fought hard, he ran with the leaders, his rider's silks were clean as a victors' should be, the others dirty and brown and beaten. But he was tired. He had won, but he had fought hard for his victory. He had shown heart and courage and toughness. Traits that Americans like. Like an American Pharaoh.

So, he came back to the baying mob, and now they were cheering, and smiling, and clapping. The mob was sated, satisfied. Their champion had emerged victorious from the battle, from the violent encounter. He was tired, but unscathed and victorious.

And even as The Roses were placed around his neck, people began to ask, people who knew horses, people who could see. They asked. *Could this be the one?*

Chapter 21

The Triple Crown. Part Two. The Preakness

The day dawned overcast. The clouds were heavy, and low, and ominous. The 140th Preakness Stakes was due to be run the afternoon of May 16, 2015, two weeks to the day after American Pharoah had emerged victorious in the Kentucky Derby. The Preakness is the older race by two years, and although its younger brother outshines it in every way now, Pimlico Race Course was still expecting a crowd of a hundred thousand to come and see the horse attempt to win the second leg of the Triple Crown.

Expectation weighed heavy on the event, on American Pharoah's connections, on the American race fans. The rain fell. The clouds sunk lower, and heavier, and darker. The dirt turned to mud. But the people came. The drink flowed. And in the infield, the kids grew raucous. And in the grandstand, those with the best seats, those with the connections and the money, they dressed in their finery, and drank their Black-Eyed Susans, and everyone waited.

Everyone knew what was coming. Everyone knew that no matter how many contests were carded that day, there was only one race, one test that mattered. *It should be a formality,* they said. *He can't be beat,* they said. Well, they can get beat. They can all get beat. There is sometimes a David to defeat Goliath, it happens. And this is a horse race, it is gladiatorial, tough, fast. Dangerous. Beautiful poetry can turn into ugly chaos in an instant.

You see the jockeys when they come into the paddock, their diminutive size a surprise to first timers—even though they knew. Their colourful silks in a myriad of hues and patterns, their jaunty walk, special to them, owed to the development of muscles of the thighs and calves, necessary to squat like a downhill skier behind the horse's mane. They can look like a little troop of players, of clowns even. And when they meet the trainers and owners, they smile and joke, and they seem as if they have not a care in the world. But if you look closer; if you look closer you will see the focus in their eyes. And if you look, you will see their demeanour change as the call for jockeys up is given. You will see a steeliness set in as they are legged up, and they lock their legs to the young

Thoroughbred. And then suddenly, they look regal, and the spectators look small and insignificant and dull compared to these men on these animals. Suddenly they look special. Suddenly everyone can see who they are, and what they can do.

Of course, for the big races, for a race like this, the jockeys room will change. The atmosphere will pervade the room, hour by hour, slowly, hardly perceptible at first, but then, as the time approaches, the riders thoughts turn to the big one. And they change out of the silks from the previous race, and their torsos are taut and lean and muscular, and for some of them, then, their scars are exposed. Some are small, some minor incident. But some are deep and terrible. Some awful battle, some moment when carnage reigned, and people and horses were hurt. They were hurt. But they recovered, and they returned to the battle. They would not be cowed or bowed. Because they are brave, because this is what they do, because this is what they feel compelled to do. Because the glory of the win, the urge for victory, is greater than the fear of the pain, for now at least.

So, they carry on time and time again, and sometimes on days like this, they get to be a part of history. Their names shall be written in the history books of the sport. And a hundred years from now, people may look and wonder who these people were, and what was life like back then.

The sky was grey, and black, and low, and wet, and the track was muddy. And as the riders prepared for the race, great, deep, heavy footsteps of thunder rocked everything.

Lightning flashed, and rain threw itself down upon the Earth. The infield was emptied of people, and when the storm lessened, the horses and jockeys paraded out onto the flooded, muddy, dirty track. Everything was grey and wet. The riders' colourful silks subdued by the wet air, by the grey sky, and in the race, by the flying mud.

He broke out of the gates well and took the lead by the first turn, his seven competitors fanned out behind him. He travelled easily through the water and mud along the backstretch and entered the home turn in command. But the time had been fast early, and the conditions were testing, and he was just a three-year-old Thoroughbred, powerful but fragile. It isn't over just because they enter the stretch in front, now it takes talent, it takes heart, it takes everything. And as the commentator was drowned out by the roaring crowd, he came, a gold and turquoise beast emerging from the primordial soup, from the water and the muddy earth from which everything was born. And each furious stride sent curtains of dirt high into the air, spraying the sky. Declaring himself its master.

And as he crossed the line, everything became one.

Chapter 22

The Bug Year: June 2015

Churchill Downs, Indiana Grand, Belterra Park

June started in the best possible way, with Jack scoring on a very fast mare by the name of Gift Receipt in a $54,000 allowance race at Churchill Downs over five furlongs on the turf—his biggest victory to date. And suddenly it was all go again.

The weather was glorious; we loved going down to the pool when we got back after racing. We would swim and lounge for a while, then take a leisurely walk to Kroger, just behind our apartment, to pick up dinner.

Kentucky is a laid-back place at the best of times, but in the summer nothing and nobody seems to be in a rush. I always thought the Irish were laid back people. But the average Kentuckian makes the typical Irishman look like an agitated, strung-out mess.

When we first arrived from the UK, I had been training racehorses for the best part of two decades. Racehorse training, when it comes down to it, is about trying to predict everything that a half ton of overfed, overexcited Thoroughbred can think of doing wrong and trying to prevent it. Professional worrier and doomsayer could be an alternative job title for a trainer. Sir Mark Prescott, always claims a happy trainer is a bad trainer.

So, we were driving into Kentucky on the first day of our new adventure, and I was probably still fretting about whether or not I had turned the oven off back in the UK, when I start to become aware that everyone else on the highway, in front, behind, and alongside me, seemed to be busy drinking coffee, smoking, and talking and texting on their phones, causing them to drift gently, and quite balletically really, from lane to lane—including the guy with the sixty-ton truck filling my rearview mirror as he bore down on me.

For months really, after we arrived, Vicky and I existed in a state of terror and disbelief. Some of the junctions were ferocious, run-the-gauntlet type affairs. Trucks were enormous and sped. Pickup trucks were huge, and you knew the drivers all had guns. There were bad parts of town, and turnoffs you missed, and traffic lights where you weren't expecting them. And the roads were black and dark at night, with streetlights nearly non-existent. And everything was big and impersonal and alien. And we felt small and insignificant and alien. Getting on and off junctions was a family affair, involving screaming, crying, praying. And me, with wild staring eyes and white knuckles locked onto the steering wheel.

Jack despaired and called us a pair of morons. And he was right. We were like a pair of cave dwellers dropped into the modern world. Driving on the other side of the road was a bit different, the junctions and road signs were a bit different, everything was just a bit different. But we could not cope at all; we couldn't get our bearings, couldn't remember routes. Jack would look at me in disbelief as I asked him for the twentieth time which turnoff we needed, usually just as we were passing it. I don't know for sure why this was, I think maybe it was a mixture of age and stress and anxiety.

With time, however, and using Jack as our guide and teacher, his parents slowly adapted. It took over a year. But now, I am pleased to say, we are as carefree, reckless, and indifferent to road safety laws as the next man. If the next man is Kentuckian.

People just don't seem to worry here; there is no nanny state here. No government signs telling you about all of the scary things that are potentially bad for you, or dangerous to do, or in other ways injurious or potentially harmful. And at first you think: *My God this place is still half wild.* But you know, on a warm June day, when all is green and sunny, and the breeze is warm, and the air smells fresh and clean, and the roads are quiet, and the horses are grazing in the paddocks under glorious giant oaks, you start to unwind, you can't help it. Living is meant to be slow and easy in Kentucky. And it is seductive. And before you know it, you are driving along with your foot out the window...

So, I don't know what I thought I was achieving by jumping up and down and fretting over Jack's results if he went a few weeks without a winner. But I began to realize (and so did Jack) that people on the Kentucky racing circuit were looking a bit askew at the crazy-acting person that was showing up everywhere all of a sudden—especially when the OCD I had suffered from as a child resurfaced in the form of rituals and silent prayers (well, I thought they were silent) before each of his races.

It was as a youngster, after my father's death, that I first developed these rituals to try and stave off misfortune. My family, instead of taking me to see a child psychologist, came up with a very novel treatment of their own, which involved laughing uproariously, pointing at me, and mocking me at every opportunity.

To their absolute astonishment this didn't seem to cure me. But being around horses did, especially when I went off at the age of seventeen to work in a racing stables. The exhilaration of riding Thoroughbreds, and the fitness and strength gained, and the expulsion of my pent-up nervous energy through hard physical work completely ridded me of my condition—until Jack began race riding day in, day out in America. But there was nothing else I could do, do you see? He was out there, on his own. And I was up there, in the stands, watching. You wouldn't want to stand by and watch from afar your child going into battle, would you?

The fretting over a lack of wins, though, was silly wasted worry. Because no one else really cared. No one else was bothered. And sure enough, after the quiet time, the winners came around again.

On the ninth and tenth of the month he picked up a couple of $30,000 maidens at Indiana, and, following a few good seconds, he then won an allowance race at Belterra Park in Ohio on another favourite mare, Abbey's Promise.

Three days later he bagged another winner at Churchill Downs, and four days after that, he rode a double at Belterra Park. Jack and I were covering a lot of miles, as he was riding mostly six days a week, in three different states. But there were winners all over the place, good purse money, sunshine, swimming pools, the mall, the movies, a nice little apartment, a very nice car.

That June we were living the dream, things were good, and somehow, someway, it seemed that everything was working out. Jack was riding plenty and becoming better known, and I was doing better, taking some pleasure, trying to chill a little bit. Trying to enjoy the American Dream.

And Vicky loved the swimming pool and the small old pickup truck she got for work! And Geri, we discovered, absolutely adored air-conditioning.

June total: 7 wins from 57 rides
Bug Year total: 49 wins from 490 rides

Chapter 23

Around Kentucky with the Bug

So, what about the bug? What does travelling around Kentucky with the bug entail?

Most days begin with breezing horses that, in the next week or two, he may be riding in races. This is both fitness training for the animal and a chance for Jack to get to know the horse—and for the horse to get to know Jack too, I suppose! And it is also an opportunity to spend some time with the trainers.

During his bug year, Jack breezed horses regularly at Keeneland, Churchill Downs, Turfway Park, Indiana Grand, Ellis Park, the Thoroughbred Training Center, and Victory Haven training centre.

If breezing at Keeneland at, say, six a.m., he would be up at five-thirty, a quick splash of water, dress, and then we would drive the ten minutes to the track. But if he was breezing at Indiana, we would be up at three-thirty a.m., and have a two and-a-half hour drive to the track. Even if he was staying around Lexington for the morning he could be breezing at two or three different training centres, so there could be mad dashes in the car between each breeze.

For the breeze itself, Jack arrives at the barn, where the horse is generally already tacked up and good to go. He will have a quick word with the trainer or their assistant, who will tell him what distance and intensity of work they want, then they will leg him up and he will be off to the track.

The track in the mornings can be a hectic place, and I have been amazed at how well the horses generally seem to take it. Horses jogging to their starting points will go clockwise around the track, pause at their appointed starting point, then turn and set off at a hack canter for a few furlongs until they get to the point three or four or five furlongs from the winning post, where the breeze is set to start. The horses know what the jock is on them for, and they can be pretty revved up and difficult to restrain until the time to cut them loose.

Once they get rolling, Jack will relax his hands, the horse will move quickly up the gears, and Jack will tuck down behind him. If it is an easy breeze, he will maintain a quiet hold of the reins, but if the trainer asks, he may push the horse out right to the finish line. Once past the finish post, the horse will gallop out for a few more furlongs before being brought to a halt, then turned and walked back off the track and straight back to the barn, where a hot walker shall take the horse and wash it down and cool it off. The whole thing may only take fifteen or twenty minutes, and Jack might jump straight up on another one and be off again.

Some days he has no breezes, most days a few, but some days he has breezed eight or nine in a morning, and that is a tough physical day's work in itself. And all those morning breezes are unpaid, it's what jockeys do to secure mounts in the afternoons.

Jockeys in North America are generally independent contractors. A rider will hire a jockey agent, and it is the agent's job to go around the barns in the morning with his rider and sell the jockey to the trainers, drum up new business, and maintain existing contacts.

For providing this service, they take twenty-five percent of their jockey's earnings! Agents are generally limited to representing no more than two riders, and this is a competitive and cutthroat business. Many agents are sterling professionals, but others seem to relish their maverick and sometimes notorious reputations. So, if you are universally disliked, totally out of shape, untrustworthy to the point that you would visit your blind old grandmother and leave with some of her household possessions, in order to finance your substance abuse problems, then congratulations! Jockey agent could be just the job for you!

After the morning breezes are done, there may be the traditional doughnuts to deliver to barns for the trainer and staff if Jack has recently ridden a winner for them, and then it is off home to check his weight.

Jack says maintaining his weight is the toughest part of his job. Like most teenage boys, he likes his food; but as a bug, he claims a weight allowance, which means the weights his horses are set to carry are even lower than the other jockeys'. He has tacked as low as 110 pounds during his bug year, and that includes the weight of the saddle and his riding clothes—all of which are created to be as light as possible, but still add four pounds—and himself, of course! To be an eighteen-year-old young man standing five feet nine and to weigh well under 110lb is very tough, physically and mentally, and we were all relieved when his weight allowance was gone.

After checking his weight, he might hit the gym for thirty minutes if he needs to lose a bit of weight, then have a wash and change. In the winter, when racing at Turfway Park, Jack will have most of the day to himself, and we'll head off to the races around three in the afternoon. But the rest of the year, there generally isn't much spare time. I will pick up a *Daily Racing Form,* and we will then sit down together in front of the computer, pull up the Equibase site, and start going through the form of his races later that day.

For each race, he'll watch a few video replays of the horse he is going to ride and form an opinion of how the horse might prefer to be ridden—up with the pace, held up early, bustled along, or ridden quietly. And he'll also look through the rest of the field to assess what the other runners will be intent on doing early in the race—the more front-runners in the field, generally the faster the pace, and you have to decide whether to alter your own tactics accordingly.

Depending on where the races are that day, we may be on the road anywhere from the ten minutes to Keeneland Racecourse, to the three hours to Ellis Park.

Once at the races, Jack is straight into the jocks room. Did I mention breakfast and lunch? No? There isn't any breakfast or lunch. Just one protein bar, except during Turfway Park, when he'll fuel up on beans and toast to prepare himself for riding late into a cold night.

The jockeys room is its own little world, and Jack, like most jockeys, likes being in there. There is plenty of banter, none of which travels outside the room. What happens in the jocks room, really does stay in the jocks room.

Todd Taylor, Jack's valet, is the man who Jack looks up to as much as any here in the USA. A good man with a ready smile, a sense of mischief in his blue eyes, and a voice like loose gravel in a cement mixer. He is a bit of a legend around these parts and merits a chapter of his own, but until the United States obscenity laws are relaxed, that is a chapter which shall remain unwritten. Todd has looked after Jack during his time here. And when Jack needs sound counsel Todd is his go-to source.

Once in the jocks room, Jack will check his weight with the clerk, then put his breeches on and do some stretching and use the jockey exerciser (a carpet covered wooden horse which they can practice pushing out and using their stick on).

After his warm-up he will go through the race program again and wait for his race while chatting with the other jocks and valets.

Come race time, his silks will be ready by his peg, courtesy of Todd, who will also get his saddle ready. While Todd takes the saddle out to the trainer and helps saddle the horse, Jack will sit down again, maybe take a sip of water, and wait to be called out to the paddock.

Out in the paddock, he has a chance to briefly greet the horse's owner, if present, and maybe discuss tactics with the trainer. Some trainers give detailed orders (Sir Mark Prescott writes a letter) whilst others just say good luck. (Some say that a bad jockey can't carry out instructions, and a good one doesn't need them—and there is probably some truth in that.)

Jack says he finds it helpful to know if the horse has any particular likes or dislikes about how it is ridden, but that it can be distracting if burdened down with a long list of instructions.

Once the "riders up" is called, the jockeys are legged up, and the horses are led out to the track and passed over to a mounted outrider, who will generally keep the horse on a lead rope during the warm-up. During this time, if the rider is not happy with the horse, if it feels sore, or if the vet feels it is sore, then it can be scratched from the race (there are always pre-race checks of the horse by a veterinarian, so this is a rare occurrence). Next, after a five-minute warm-up, the horses are loaded into the starting gate.

This is a tense time for horse, rider, and stall handlers. The aim is to get an average of eight highly strung horses, who are wound like a spring and know what the stalls mean, into the gate quickly and safely, and then away. Most of the time it goes surprisingly smoothly, sometimes it doesn't, and stalls accidents can be scary and nasty. Everyone is relieved when they are off.

There is a technique to getting horses out of the gate quickly, how the horse is positioned, how the jockey holds the reins, how he is sat, anticipating the starter. Being fast away is paramount in the States where early speed is vital, as the slow horses get dirt kicked in their faces, which can discourage them. In the States, the first two furlongs of the race are generally the fastest, and the last two generally the slowest.

Once out of the gate, position is the aim. Trying to situate the horse where you had planned before the race, or if the start has not gone to plan, or if the pace of the race is different than expected, then deciding instantly how to adapt.

Through the race, the aim is to get the horse to relax and run smoothly and evenly, which encourages it to breathe well and conserve energy until they round the home turn, and it is time to race for the finish line.

Jack has been riding race finishes since he was a tiny kid. Firstly, on a bale of hay with reins hooked around it. Then on his little pony, drilling the poor startled beast up the gallops! Then on the jockey exerciser at the British National Horseracing Museum, where the now sadly passed, lovely, Alfie Westwood would encourage Jack. And in spite of being well over seventy years of age and having had a hip and knee replacement, Alfie could not resist popping up on it himself—just to show Jack how it was done! He always said Jack was his tip for the top and would be very proud of him.

From there Jack joined the British Racing School and was tutored more on Equicizers, and then we bought one for the yard, which he was constantly on too. So, if there is one thing Jack Gilligan can do, it is push a horse out to the line and look good doing it!

After the race, the victor heads to the winner's circle, while the rest of the runners are unsaddled on the track. If he's not in the circle, Jack passes his saddle back to his valet, and then gives a quick rundown of how the race went to the trainer; this is his chance to relate to him or her, his impressions and thoughts of what might possibly be done, regarding distance, class, race tactics, or equipment, to help the horse possibly win next time. Then he has a quick march back to the jocks room and gets ready to do it all over again.

Some days he may only have one or two rides, sometimes he rides the full card of eight or nine races. When the day is done, he has a wash and shower, and thirty minutes after his last ride, we're back in the car for the journey home. After we got a car of our own, this was when Jack would get his driving lessons from me. He had taken lessons back home, so was already pretty good, but since we drove over seventy thousand miles that bug year, and he probably drove at least fifteen thousand of them, he at least got in plenty of practice!

Home after racing means one thing to Jack. Dinner! Five nights a week, it is sensible home-cooked food with vegetables. Once or twice a week, we eat out or get carryout. Every night he eats a good meal and follows it with a bowl of ice cream. Then it's either a movie or a bit of time with his headphones on and his iPad. The post-dinner entertainment depends on what time we got home, which could be anywhere from three p.m. if riding an early race at Keeneland, to midnight if in the last at Turfway.

Then to bed, and repeat the next day, up to six days a week. There is normally no racing on Jack's circuit on a Monday except on major holidays—and that is much appreciated, and I think it is madness that the UK does not do the same thing. I think asking jockeys to race ride seven days a week must be tremendously draining on them, especially if they are enduring a poor run. That day off gives the jockey a chance to recharge physically and mentally.

Each day is demanding. It is a serious business. Each race is intense and physical. Each race has risk. Each race also offers reward.

Jockeys in the USA receive lower riding fees than in the UK (roughly seventy dollars versus one hundred plus pounds) but the higher prize money in the US more than compensates for that—as long as you are winning. A jockey receives ten percent of the winning owners' prize money, which can amount to a few hundred dollars in the cheapest races at the smallest tracks, up to tens of thousands of dollars for a major stakes win. Second and third percentages do not amount to much, except in the more valuable races, so a jockey in North America has to be winning, preferably at least one or two a week.

To give an example, as I am writing this, Jack has just collected his checks (which are issued to the riders by the track each week) from riding at Indiana Grand and Churchill Downs last week. He only had three rides at Indiana, but one of them won a $30,000 allowance; his check was a bit over $2,000. His check at Churchill was also a little over $2,000 for one win in a smaller race from sixteen rides.

A top-tier rider in the USA can average a weekly pay cheque in excess of twenty thousand dollars. That's pretty nice money, but a third of that goes to their agent and valet, and then there is the tax man. It can still be a very good living, though, being a jockey. You know what they say... it's a bug's life!

Chapter 24

Baffert's Hair

About a week after American Pharoah had won the Preakness Stakes, I was queuing for a coffee in the Starbucks just around the corner from Churchill Downs. Ahead of me in the line, I noticed a neatly dressed silver-haired man, hair grown a certain length and with that familiar, shall we call it, say, the Baffert flap? The trademark curtain of hair that falls down over the right side of his forehead. Now I had never met Bob Baffert, American Pharoah's trainer, up close and personal, so I didn't really know if he was short or tall. I just thought this man's features, from my angle slightly behind him, fitted. Vicky was at a table nearby, waiting for me to collect the drinks, so I caught her eye and gestured while mouthing silently, "Is that Bob Baffert?" She took a look and shrugged and silently mouthed back, "I don't think so."

This was a conundrum. Would I have liked the opportunity to say hello and to congratulate the man who had just trained the winner of the first two legs of the Triple Crown? Of course I would. Did I want to embarrass myself in the middle of Starbucks by congratulating the local bank manager on his outstanding handling of American Pharoah? Not really. So I ummed and ahhed, and in the end, he ordered his coffee and he left.

Later that day, during media coverage of American Pharoah's buildup to the Triple Crown, we found out that whilst the Pharoah was at Churchill Downs, Bob Baffert was back in California at that time, supervising the rest of his powerful string of horses.

This worried me a lot. Because it meant that somewhere out there, someone must have gone into their barber's and asked for a "Baffert" or a "Bob" or a full-on "Bob Baffert please!" Firstly, I had always supposed that this was a patented haircut, available only to the great man himself. Secondly, it is a haircut of such improbable appearance, so science fiction–like in its presentation, that I found it hard to believe that another man could carry it off like Bob. The odds against two such men existing seemed too extreme to me.

And what if American Pharoah wins the Triple Crown? What then? His face will be everywhere—and I'm not talking about the horse. What if there is a rush of men who see the great trainer's magnificent haircut and decide, "That's the one for me!" What if barbers up and down the country have customers flocking in, demanding a Baffert? Not silver-haired, cosmopolitan, urbane gentlemen, but half-bald, overweight, middle-aged men. Men whose T-shirts don't quite cover their bellies, ginger-haired men, burly rednecks.

It would be a disaster. To be faced with such unedifying tributes to his own masterful look would surely cause him to seek an alternative hairstyle. And this would be a disaster too. For I am convinced that, like Samson, much of Bob Baffert's success is down to his haircut.

You see, if you go down to the track in the mornings, what you will notice is that although there are many different trainers, all their horses are doing the same thing galloping around in circles on the track. There is sometimes a degree of mystique attached to the art of racehorse training, so I shall now clear it away and explain to you what it really entails. And it is this; the trainer arrives in the morning, and sends the horse to the track to gallop around. And if it's not sore that evening, then the following morning he does the same thing. And the trainer repeats this day in, day out. Until it is sore. And then he calls the owner to give them the unfortunate news.

So, you see, if all these trainers are doing the same thing, why is there only one of them who keeps threatening to win the Triple Crown? What has he got that the others don't? That haircut is what stands out to me.

So, although we are all rooting (I know) for American Pharoah's triumph in the final leg of the Triple Crown, I fear it could be a personal disaster for the inimitable trainer himself, should he succeed.

I only hope I am wrong, and that it is just the caffeine talking…

Chapter 25

The Triple Crown. Part Three. The Belmont Stakes

I was at Indiana Grand Racing and Casino on Saturday, June 6, 2015. The day of the 147th running of the Belmont Stakes. The day American Pharoah was to face his greatest test.

The mile and a half route, over the large Belmont Park oval, is an extreme distance on dirt, and there was little guarantee on pedigree that the Kentucky Derby and Preakness winner could last out the extra two furlongs. Further than he had ever run before. Further than any of them had ever run before. For the eight runners due to go to post shortly before seven p.m. New York time, this was going to be the most exhausting day of their lives.

I have spent a lot of time at Indiana Grand. Jack rides there often during the summer. It is a long drive there, and when you arrive, it is uninspiring, strictly business, more about the casino than the racing. Hardly anyone watches the racing, except on Saturdays, when they race in the evening. Then people come and eat barbecue and drink beer and bet the ponies. This Saturday, though, you couldn't move. All of Indiana was there. They were there to watch the Belmont Stakes.

About an hour before the big race I went down into the casino; it was humming, but I was able to grab a lone stool at the sports bar. From there I could watch the boy race and also watch Belmont Park.

The sky was blue in New York, and due to crowd concerns, for the first time, the venue had limited itself to ninety thousand tickets sold. They were all taken before the day of the event. I had seen the crowd before for the Belmont. I had seen them before with a

Triple Crown contender. Crazy crowds, loud, boisterous, drunk, hollering and shouting. Wild. And I had seen the disappointment before, when the wrong horse won, when the Triple Crown went unclaimed for another year. It had been unclaimed for thirty-seven years now.

I got talking to the guy next to me at the bar, the way you do. I asked him what he liked for the big one, what he thought about American Pharoah.

"That horse won't stay!" he exclaimed aggressively. "I've taken the field against him, exactas, trifectas, superfectas. That horse won't win today!"

I looked down in front of him; there was a tall pile of tickets next to his beer. I didn't say anything. The man seemed agitated, maybe he had staked too much, maybe he had drunk too much. Maybe both.

Except for the distance and the weather, the race was a rerun of the Preakness. American Pharoah slightly missed the break but had secured the lead by the first turn. Along the backstretch, I marvelled again at his stride, so powerful and fluent and long, and I knew then that a stride like that would break his competitors, before it faltered itself.

He turned into the long Belmont homestretch on a tight rein still, and Frosted made an attempt to draw up to him, to challenge him, to make a race of it. There was no use, though, he was too good. He was born too good. And as his rider shook the reins at him and sent him to the wire, he opened up and lengthened his stride, and he extended his lead, and the crowd was delirious, and the commentator was screaming and hoarse with excitement, and the bar erupted. And as he passed the wire, the first Triple Crown winner since 1978, the man next to me was crying "No! No! NO!" in despair.

There have been over seven hundred thousand Thorough-bred colt foals born in North America since the crop in which Affirmed, the last Triple Crown winner, was born in 1975. He was ridden by a quiet, modest, charming kid from Kentucky. "The Kentucky Kid." He was just eighteen years old when he won the Triple Crown on Affirmed. The same age my son, also a jockey, was when American Pharoah won the Triple Crown. But my son was riding lesser horses at Indiana that night, he is waiting for his shot, for his big horse still. But he is young. It isn't often you get a shot to star as young as Steve Cauthen was all those years ago. It was the rider who seemed born for greatness in the 1978 Triple Crown series. In the 2015 Triple Crown, it was the horse who was born for greatness.

American Pharoah has just been better than the seven hundred thousand other colts that came along since Affirmed. There had been plans for all of them when they were born. Hopes. Dreams. Some were realized, to a lesser or greater extent. Many were disappointments, failures who could not live up to the dreams placed on them, unwittingly, unknowingly. They tried but they could not succeed.

And how many people were born in that time, how many dreams did they have, how many succeeded, and how many failed? What of my friend at the bar? What dreams had his parents had for him when he was born, what aspirations were there?

Or were there none? Was he cursed from birth? Did no one love him properly, or care for him deeply, or dream for him greatly? Was he destined to be miserable, to hope for failure in others? Or had he tried? Had he tried like American Pharoah's opponents, but was found wanting? Did he find that he just couldn't fulfill his dreams in any measure? That he didn't have what it took, that he just couldn't make it?

Greatness strikes rarely. It is not failure to not win. Gallant Frosted in second was not a failure. The seventeen talented horses and riders strung out behind the great one in the Kentucky Derby were not failures. They were not failures because they were still trying, still fighting, still in the game, playing the game. Making the game.

But people shouldn't bet against the great ones, equine or human. The great ones may lose battles here and there, but, in the end, eventually, they tend to win the wars. That is why most people cheer for them, and love them, and applaud them. Like I did.

And it made the hair on the back of my neck stand up as he crossed the line, because finally, American Pharoah, after all those years, after all that waiting. He really was *The One*.

Chapter 26

Thinking Freely

If you are a reasonably intelligent person and possess any sort of a romantic soul and sense of wonder at the world we live in, then it is almost inevitable that, at certain times, you will be found, incapacitated, sat on a stool in a bar, talking what a sober man would call horseshit.

The existential powers of hard liquor are required sometimes for the thinking man to fully absorb and analyse at a conceptual level his existence, as he journeys through his time on this planet. This small spinning ball dancing fawnishly around the uncaring, giant, burning, roaring sun. One rocky planet, one sea of blue, and clouds of white, and mountains of green, speeding through a cold, black void of nothingness. If you have ever looked through a telescope at planets such

169

as Mars or Jupiter, you will know how very alone they hang there out in space. How grey and dead they look.

Are we alone in the universe? No. Are we not proof that alien life exists? That alien civilizations can exist. That from tiny organisms can emerge creatures able to harness nature's powers for their own purposes, and hence, even to shake off the ultimate mother's possessiveness, the weighty attraction of the planet they miraculously sprang from.

These are the thoughts your mind takes you to when freed from its daily burden of the mundane day-to-day necessities and duties that the sober are tied up around.

So take a shot. Have a tequila, a scotch on the rocks, down a margarita, sip a golden rum, enjoy a boilermaker, a whisky sour, or a gimlet. Swill a frozen vodka, knock back a cold one, or contemplate while downing a bourbon, or a Lynchburg lemonade. Champagne will get you where you want to go—and ouzo where you don't. A mojito in the summer, a hot toddy in the winter. The highball, the white Russian, an old-fashioned, a martini. They have all been my companion, from time to time.

Stay away from the top shelf, they say. And they are right. They who have never thought deeply, never felt deeply, never hurt deeply, never loved deeply. They, who exist momentarily on this hurtling, spinning uncontrollable projectile—how do we even stay stuck on this bastard? Gravity my arse! They, who have never given thought to the mind-numbing, mind-bending, mind-twisting, miraculous ridiculousness of our existence. Of our ability to question our existence, of our ability to ask God's questions.

For we are the mind of God, are we not? We have sprung into existence from nowhere, from this nothingness, this universe. Our bodies formed from the ashes of stars that lived for aeons, and have been dead for aeons now. When we think, we are the universe thinking and wondering and questioning. If that doesn't call for a drink, I don't know what does!

So, should you mow the fucking lawn whilst worrying about your chances for a promotion? Or should you roll up your sleeves, sit down at a bar, order a stiff one, and get on with thinking about the important stuff—that the universe gave you a brain to think about.

Chapter 27

Came the Dark Horse

He was the first Thoroughbred I ever bought. I purchased him at auction on one bid for four hundred and fifty guineas. And they threw in the devil for free.

A neat little yearling colt with a coat as black as the coals that stoke the fires of hell. "Cheap, small, and common" would be the dismissive consensus of the experts. Perhaps they forgot that his line went back to Northern Dancer, and that Northern Dancer, champion racehorse, legendary sire, was also passed over as too small as a yearling by the experts.

Black horses sometimes seem to have a bit more temperament than the average racehorse. And this little yearling turned into a blackguard two-year-old. Strong willed, unwilling to submit, acknowledging no one as his master. He would rear, and spin, and buck, and run backward as often as forward; he would dive off the gallops, plunging. And he grew big and muscular and strong, and he had eyes like an eagle's, predatory, unafraid. Never afraid. Never shying or running from a sudden noise or a startling scene. He was the Alpha of alpha males.

Eventually, somehow, he accepted enough of what I asked him to do that I thought he was ready to race. It was a big day for me. My first ever runner in a race. A horse I had bought and broken and ridden and trained and groomed and fed and cared for. I had clung on when he'd tried to throw me, and I had escaped most of his open-mouthed lunges at my arms and dodged most of his raised, jabbing, threatening hind legs, which would arc and slowly circle, like a Yankees' batsman waiting to let loose his biggest swing.

He took two strides out onto the track with the jockey on his back, and he reared to his fullest height. The jockey was dislodged, and the blackguard took off. The race was delayed while we sped around the course in the back of a Range Rover to catch him. I found him on the far side; he had his head down eating grass. *Fuck you,* he said. *You don't own me. I call the shots here.* He never did misbehave on the racetrack again. He was just letting me know that it was his choice to race, not mine.

But boy, could he run. Just a month after that debacle, he disposed of a useful field of two-year-old maidens at Royal Windsor Racecourse. And then, just fading late after setting a blistering early pace, he finished fifth in the richest two-year-old handicap of the year. He was clocked travelling at forty-three miles an hour that day, with the rider sat back hauling on the reins against him.

For the next two years, this dark beast and I fought for dominance. He became even tougher to deal with, dangerous sometimes. I was younger and braver then, and experienced with Thoroughbreds, so mostly I didn't get too scared. Mostly. But he kept racing; he channelled that aggression, that inner rage, that desire for dominance into performance on the racetrack. You could see it in the way he stretched at the gallop, his head horizontal, pushing himself to the limit, every ounce of him determined to best his foes.

He rewarded us with strings of valiant efforts in good races at the top racetracks in the country. Newmarket, Ascot, Haydock, York, we went to them all, pitching him against expensive horses from the big, established stables, beating more of them than beat us. Giving us great excitement, great days, great moments. Cheering, shouting, punching the air, hugging, congratulating, laughing. Adrenaline-fuelled celebrations.

By four he had become dangerous to be around. A brooding monster, stalking around his caged stall. Malevolent. Looking for a fight. He would rear in his stable and put his feet against the wall, to look down with blazing eyes on his cowering neighbour in the next stall. He would pick up his feed manger and hurl it over the wall out into the walkway.

His teeth were weapons now; a rag or a stick was needed to engage them whenever he was handled. He was powerful now. A magnificent beast. An alpha male in his prime, with an alpha male's aggression.

I had him castrated that spring. It is a bigger job when they are older, a lot of blood is spilt. But he recovered well. He still remained a handful, willful, tough and ornery, and still aggressive—except with Jack. When the boy walked up to him, the horse would lower his big head and allow him to push his toy stethoscope up into one of his velvet nostrils, and he would allow him to stroke his silken nose, and his ears would be pricked the whole time, seemingly mesmerized by this tiny child.

For the rest of us, though, the ears stayed pinned back. But at least he stopped rearing, and the anger, the rage at his captivity, subsided slightly, and he continued to channel his aggression into his races. Indeed, he even raced better, year after year, winning and placing all over the country. Until, at the age of seven, he won his first stakes race. The JRA Nakayama Rous Stakes at Newmarket racetrack. Our home. He was 50/1 in the morning betting, and he won by a nose. I remember waiting the eternal wait for the result of the photo finish. "First, number ten, Rushcutter Bay..." I choked up, couldn't talk as people grabbed me. It is still etched in my soul all these years later. Something I had done, something I had achieved. No money, no connections, no father. Yet somehow, someway, I was standing there as a trainer in the winner's enclosure for a major race, at one of the most historic racetracks in the world. It was nothing in the great scheme of things of course. But it was everything to me.

And the best was yet to come. The following spring, he followed up in the Group 3 Palace House Stakes, back on the Rowley Mile, on 2000 Guineas Day. The spring sun shining, tens of thousands of spectators, and legendary jockey Mick Kinane in the saddle.

He did it well that day, a flash of black tearing down on the slighter, grey filly in the lead; he thundered past her, opening up as he hit the final hill. The dominant winner. At that moment, the highest rated sprinter in Europe. Champagne. Dreams of Royal Ascot. Looking forward to Longchamp on Arc Day for his first Group 1 contest. All that he gave us in return for a bucket of feed a few times a day.

He never won another race though. The urge had dimmed a little. He was getting older, passing his prime. The fire that raged inside consumed him less. He was still tough, still trouble, still full of life. But other horses could win the races now. He had fought enough, tried enough, pushed himself enough. He had ruptured enough blood vessels in his lungs, trying to fight for an extra inch or two of flight. He had returned after races with enough of his own blood spilling from his nose. He had tasted victory and defeat enough times now to know those two imposters.

It is over ten years since he ran his last race. I wonder sometimes if he ever remembers. If he ever relives those moments, if they stay with him, as they have stayed with me. Does he think of those days, when he was in his prime, with pride?

Or does he remember being enslaved? Being taken from his mother on that Welsh mountainside he was born and raised on, and sold as "lot 1167, a brown colt." His mother and father, and their mother and father listed on the page…a worthless pedigree to produce a worthless horse…the mare shouldn't have been bred from said the experts. Sold to the young man with the equally damnable pedigree on one bid, for four hundred and seventy pounds. Two longshots brought together. Two strong-willed young males. Each as obstinate as the other.

He was my whale; I was his Ahab. I was the slave master; he was the slave. He fought his enslavement, but I bent him to my will. I had to, you see. There was no other choice for him. He was born a Thoroughbred, an artificial breed, selected for speed, selected for man's sport. He was magnificent, because that is what we bred him to be. So, he could be a racehorse, or he could be nothing. And in the end, he chose to race, to roll like thunder.

But sometimes he haunts me now.

It is twenty-three years since I first saw that small yearling. And I spent nearly every day with him over the next two decades. But I haven't seen him for three years now. And he is four thousand miles away from me. And neither of us are young anymore.

Sometimes now I dream of him being free, a magnificent wild stallion roaming with his herd of mares, mares he had won by fighting for them, by subduing other, lesser foes. And because I am older now, I see him with his offspring. All of his sons and daughters, all of them beautiful, and proud like him. All of them running together, free like the wind. His superior genes passed on to those descendants, ensuring he would live on, that he would shape the future in some way, that his magnificence would last.

And then one day, when he was past his prime, he would be bested in battle. And he would find somewhere to lay down with his wounds, alone, to die on that mountainside. A wild unconquerable beast, who had lived as God had intended him to live. And was to die as God intended him to die. Unbowed, untamed. Unnamed.

Chapter 28

The Bug Year: July 2015

Ellis Park, Indiana Grand, Del Mar

By July, even the ice cubes were sweating in Kentucky. Days were languid and blue. And when you stepped outside of your air-conditioned apartment, or car, or store, the heat would hit you in the face like you had opened an oven door. And I thought, *This is plenty hot.* But then I went to Ellis.

Ellis Park racetrack is where the Kentucky circuit races in July and August. Affectionately known as the Pea Patch, it is located one hundred and ninety-six miles west of Lexington, on the western Kentucky border with Indiana. The border itself is marked by the Ohio River, which dissects the states and lays up against the racetrack. Its low-lying situation, midwestern location, and the proximity of the river make Ellis Park, without a doubt, the sweatiest racetrack I have ever encountered. I swear, Ellis Park is so hot that sometimes you wish you could go to hell, just to cool off.

In truth, although you could still see why many horsemen talked fondly of days gone by, it was, by the time Jack went to race there, a bit of a shabby, run-down, and not very clean venue. And that, together with the long journey to and from and the meltingly hot temperatures, meant that I never really took the place to heart—even after Jack won the very first race, win number fifty! On the very first day of the meet.

With racing three days a week at Ellis, and two or three days a week at Indiana, we were clocking up around two thousand miles a week in the car now. And the swimming pool —now I needed it most—I didn't often get to enjoy. The weeks became a blur of long journeys, blazing hot sun, service stations, junk food, and ordinary racing.

But business is business, and from his victory in the first race on the first day, Jack went on to ride a couple more winners in the second week. Week three yielded three seconds, and a good third in the stakes on Saturday, but no victories.

The following week, though, started with a win… And then we were off to Del Mar in San Diego for the weekend!

A couple of three-year-olds that Jack had won maidens on at Indiana had been taken to race at Del Mar's famous summer meet by their Californian trainer. And she had kindly told Jack that he could ride them there if he liked. It was a great opportunity to go out and experience West Coast racing, so he gladly accepted—and if I had gone all the way to Mahoning Valley just to be nosey, I wasn't going to miss this! So, after riding a few at Ellis Park on Friday we flew out from the nearby Henderson airport, and on to San Diego via Chicago.

Del Mar was very cool. The Spanish-style grandstand, palm trees, lovely horses, and beautiful people, all set off by the cool, sparkling blue Pacific Ocean just beyond the track. It was glamorous and busy and fun. And I tried to keep as much food as possible off my clothes. Plus, on his first mount, the filly Taylor Lane, just for a moment, it looked like he might pull off an almighty upset. As it was, she ran well, looked like she was going to challenge for a place, but tired late. Afterwards, back in the weighing room, top jockey Mike Smith went through Jack's ride with him and told him he gave her a perfect route, which pleased Jack nearly as much as a win would have. We found everyone at the track super friendly and Jack, I know, would like to go back if the opportunity arose again.

Although our jaunt had cost him a winner back at Ellis, it was great fun to go, very interesting, and a day off on Sunday, spent splashing around in the ocean, was just what we both needed to freshen us up.

Forty-eight hours on from swimming in the Pacific, Jack was riding out to the post parade at Indiana Grand for the first of two days of racing there. The first couple on the first day didn't amount to much, but his first mount on the second day was amongst the favourites, and we thought it had a decent chance.

I never miss the start of one of his races. My eyes are locked on the screen, anxiously watching, hardly breathing, one second willing the horse to run well, the next just praying safe passage. Negotiating with God.

This day, for some reason, I looked down at the race program just as they let the horses go. And when I looked up, I couldn't find Jack. Fairly unconcerned, I started scanning for his silks to find his position, but I couldn't see them, so then I counted the riders and realized one was missing, and I went a bit numb, and then I saw his horse racing with the field, without him, and I realized something must have happened at the start.

Falls out of the gate can be serious, but because the horses have not reached a full gallop often they are not. There was no audible race commentary in the bar, sometimes I prefer it that way, so I was running out of the casino toward the track when my phone rang. It was Vicky, in tears.

"Is he up?" she cried, beside herself. I replied I didn't know and was trying to ask her what happened as I ran out onto the track apron. And then I heard the commentator say the rider was still down, and it didn't look good. And I was distraught and lost and helpless.

The horse had stumbled coming out of the gate. When they stumble their noses will go down into the dirt in an effort to try and maintain their footing. But it happens so fast that the rider cannot react; the horse's big shoulders dip down, and the stretching of the head and neck pulls the reins forward together with the rider holding them. The jockey is usually propelled forward and flipped over the horse's head, down into the dirt, like a judo throw. Fast and hard. And, as often as not, the horse will run over them, trampling them, kicking them accidentally as they recover and gallop off.

The stalls handlers were with him in an instant; Jack lay prostrate on the track as the ambulance arrived. But then he moved. And he rolled over, and he gingerly picked himself up and dusted some dirt off himself. And he walked away, winded and bruised and pissed off. And I walked away, scared and sick. And his mother, at home, cried hard for many different reasons.

July total: 4 wins from 56 rides
Bug Year total: 53 wins from 546 rides

Chapter 29

The Pea Patch

Summers in Kentucky are hot and sultry. And nowhere in Kentucky is hotter or sultrier than Ellis Park racetrack in July and August.

Dade Park racetrack, as it was originally called, held its first race meet for Thoroughbred horses on November 18, 1922, in the heyday of the Roaring Twenties. Overseen by the specially formed Green River Jockey Club, the initial ten-day meet was intended as a stopover for horses travelling south by rail to New Orleans for the winter. It proved, however, too brief to be financially viable, and the Green River Jockey Club filed for bankruptcy just three years later. Subsequently that same year, a businessman by the name of James Ellis purchased the track and oversaw the facility until his death in 1956. Under his leadership, totalisator wagering was introduced, and a new grandstand was built. And in 1954, the facility was renamed Ellis Park racetrack in his honour.

Over the years and decades that followed, Ellis Park experienced changes in fortunes and changed hands several times, but kept racing uninterrupted, year in, year out, until in 2006, the track was purchased by current owner Mr. Ron Geary. For Mr. Geary, his motives for purchase seem to have been as much emotional as financial. He is a well-known horseplayer and, after his purchase, he spoke of his dream of establishing Ellis Park as the "Saratoga of the West."

Our first experience of Ellis, was on the morning of the July 2, 2015. I had driven Jack 190 miles west of Lexington to the "Pea Patch," as it is colloquially known (on account of the field of beans grown in the infield), to breeze some horses before the first day of the new meet in two days' time.

The journey, although long, was pleasant enough. Take the I-64 west from Lexington, follow it through Louisville, and keep going. It was a quiet drive, with gentle turns and rises and rolling hills and expanses of woodland interspersed with fields and small farms.

The racetrack itself is situated right beside the Ohio River, and although it is a Kentucky track, it actually sits on the northern (Indiana) side of the river; apparently it claims its Kentucky citizenship from a 1790s state border line. It is found through a clearing of trees and sits amid open farmland in as rural, tranquil, and ageless a spot as you could imagine.

It is the sort of place where you should turn off your watch, never mind your phone.

The sweltering summer heat, moistened by the grand but silent Ohio River, felt like it had sapped modern life from the place. There was a feeling of inertia, of silent stillness. Movement felt incongruous, like a fly crawling across a work by Constable.

The horses and riders, dotted here and there, were gliding along the dirt, dreamlike and surreal, small and silhouette-like against the shimmering background of fields and mighty birch trees. Even the golden, heavy sun, sat low in the sky, seemed to be just watching too.

I had heard much about the old-fashioned charm of Ellis, so after dropping Jack off on the backstretch, I was interested to go and see the facility for myself. As I approached from the rear, there seemed to be little to distinguish the grandstand from many other small racetracks we had visited here; it was tall, rectangular, and shoebox like. Walking around to the track apron, I could view the frontage, and, aside from some ornate pillars—which were a nice touch—there was again little to get excited about. It was maybe five stories high, with the top couple of levels enclosed in glass to provide trackside dining in air-conditioned comfort.

When I walked down into the ground floor of the grandstand, however, I began to see. The thoroughfare on ground level was designed to resemble a small, quaint, old-fashioned Main Street. On one side was a row of rooms—a bar, souvenir shop, horsemen's center—and the frontage to each was decorated with stained glass and wrought iron, and each fashioned as a little store in a parade and running outside the parade of mini stores was a row of old-fashioned streetlamps. It was a wonderful idea, and I expect we have Mr. Ellis to thank for it, and it should have been marvellous. But it wasn't, because the thoroughfare was dank, and patchy, and not freshly painted, and not fragrant, and frankly, it didn't seem very clean. *They have a lot of work to do in twenty-four hours,* I thought as I ventured up onto the second-floor terrace to watch the boy breeze.

The terrace again was old-fashioned and quaint, but it was also peeling paint and rusting, and again, looked like it could do with a good wash. And then I sat down and gazed out at the track, and "idyllic" would be the only word you could use. As a scene of a summer morning at a country racetrack deep in the heartland of America, well, it was just how you would imagine it. The white rails and beige dirt in the foreground. The horses and riders, in ones and twos, skimming by. The lush greenery. The long, low barns in the background, and the giant beautiful birch trees, standing here and there, tall and expansive and ageless. I kept expecting Rhett Butler to ride into view. It looked too good to be true. And it was.

It took me a while, because I was soaking in, not just the view, but the being there, just me in the stand, in the summer silence, waiting to see the boy speed by, tucked behind a flowing mane. And I am gazing about, lazily, looking at the scrubland to the inner of the main track, and inside that to the field of beans—which makes me think of another Jack—and I gaze back to the scrubland, and then back to the main dirt track. And then back to the scrubland again. And my heart briefly stops. And I realize that I am looking at the turf track. *This cannot be!* I thought. This was not a turf racetrack; it was just an untidy rug of coarse, long, wild-looking grass relieved by patches of bare soil and bushes—yes, bushes!—of weeds. In two days, my son and his colleagues were going to be expected to race around this? I couldn't believe it.

And so, without thinking really, I found myself ducking under the rail and making my way across the main track, and I noticed then that where the horses' hooves struck, they kicked off the dirt down to the clay base. It wasn't so much a dirt track as a clay road with a meagre amount of dirt sprinkled upon it. I was horrified, and my stomach felt cold inside as I ducked under another rail and onto the inner turf track.

It really was as bad as it looked from afar. It was rutted in places, and bare, and overgrown weeds were everywhere. And in the UK, there would not have been the remotest possibility of racing on it. But it wouldn't even have got that far because tracks are inspected for safety over there. And here, unbelievably, I began to realize they must not be.

And it was while I was in this stupor, gazing openmouthed around me, walking the turf, trying to avoid the ruts and the bushes of weeds, that I nearly got myself thrown out of the meet before it had even started.

It was the outrider who caught up with me first, halting from a canter about ten feet from me on the other side of the rails. "What are you doing?!" he wailed plaintively.

"Walking the track," I replied distractedly, eyes still on the turf.

"You can't be out here when they're training!" he exclaimed. "Get out of there!"

"But they're not training on this, are they?" I said, pointing down to the grass. "It's not very good is it?"

"It doesn't matter, get out of there!" he shouted.

And so I made my way under the rail and across the dirt. And then I was met by an official who roared up in a truck. And he didn't look too thrilled to be meeting me for the first time either.

"Who are you?" he spluttered. "What do you think you're doing out there? You can't go out there when they are training! Are you a horseman?"

I explained that indeed I had trained for seventeen years in Europe, and that over there it was quite common to walk the training grounds while they were in use. And I was terribly sorry for any alarm, but my son was to ride here this summer, and I had noticed that the turf track appeared a little, er, unkempt?

He looked doubtfully at me, and I'm not sure he actually thought I was all there, if you get my drift (I have that effect on people sometimes), but he let me off with a warning to behave myself, and I was free to go.

After his breezes, Jack had to walk down and meet me in the car at the stable entrance as the official in the truck was still keeping a stern eye on me, so I thought it best not to try and sneak in without a valid pass.

"Why are you parked here?" he asked as we pulled away to head home. So, I explained the saga to him. "I thought so," he said.

"How did you know?" I enquired.

"Well, I was with the outrider getting ready to breeze by the far turn, and he pointed to you and said, 'Who the fuck is that out there!!??'

"And what did you say?" I asked.

"I said, 'I don't know…just some idiot.'" And we laughed and laughed.

So, they mowed the grass, and although the tracks were blisteringly fast, and in spite of my misgivings, the meet went fine and mostly safely, which was the main thing. And people came, and some days the place was bustling, and there was an outdoor bar to enjoy a drink, and there were novelty races involving miniature dogs which were hilarious chaos. But the place still wasn't very clean. And the food wasn't good. And after all I had been told about her, Ellis was a disappointment when I met her.

I think it was a bit like going with an old friend to visit the home of someone who had been a beauty in her day. And your friend, who as a youngster was obviously keen on her, has told you how great this person is and how much you will like her.

But when you meet her, you see that she is in decline. That her skin is lined, and her makeup is askew, and her clothes are old and mismatched, and she isn't tending to herself as she should. But there is still something about her. And you see old pictures on the wall, from when she was young and beautiful, from when she made young men dream and smile and gaze with pleasure and wistfulness. And you know what your friend is seeing.

And I think that is the Ellis people were telling me about. They still recall the days when she was painted and lovingly laden with fresh flowers. And was fresher, like the people themselves. And they still think of her as she was then. They remember that when she was beautiful so were they, and they remember happy, wonderful days spent together and they thought that they would all be like this forever.

So, they tell me about this beauty because that is who, in their mind's eye, they still see. They don't see the cracks like I do, the signs of age, of slipping, of decline. And maybe it would be wrong of me to say that this is not so anymore, that their eyes deceive them. Maybe that would be wrong.

But to say that this once beautiful old lady deserves to be bathed, and her clothes freshly painted, and flowers laid all around for her, so she can be lovely once more…I think it would be all right to mention that to her friends.

Chapter 30

Old Del Mar

On July 25th 2015 Jack and I took a car, took a plane, took another plane and another car, and we found ourselves in old Del Mar.

The morning before, I had driven Jack the hour and a quarter to Churchill Downs from our home in Lexington to breeze for a couple of trainers. From there, we drove another hour and a half to Henderson, Kentucky, where Jack had a couple of rides at Ellis Park, and then we flew out of nearby Evansville airport to Chicago, and from there, on to San Diego.

We landed in San Diego around ten-thirty at night, and the view on the left as we came in was impressive, zooming past a feast of futuristic glass skyscrapers and neon lights. We picked up our luggage, and picked up our car, and made the thankfully short drive to our hotel in the small pretty coastal town of La Jolla. We were in California!

And it didn't take us long to realize what that meant. On our first morning there, we were picking up some basics from the local supermarket when a six-foot-tall, athletic, young black man walked past me in the aisle wearing a rather nice red cocktail dress. The thing is, though, that everyone around us seemed so individual in their appearance that Jack didn't even notice him go by. He wouldn't have gone unnoticed in Indiana, I can tell you that much.

Del Mar racetrack was the brainchild of ex–American football star William Quigley. He thought San Diego could do with a racecourse, and he approached Bing Crosby, who was a big race fan and owned a string of racehorses himself, to see if he would get involved. Well he did, big time—and he brought in some of his friends too.

By the time the racetrack was ready to open its doors in 1937, the list of board members and officials included Bing Crosby himself, Pat O'Brien, Gary Cooper, and Oliver Hardy! It's who you know…And come opening day, Bing and Pat were there at the gates personally shaking hands with the race fans as they entered the track. Before the first race Bing sang "Old Del Mar," and it is still played each day of the meet. Del Mar racetrack quickly became a playground for many of Hollywood's biggest stars. Clark Gable, Ava Gardner, Bob Hope, Betty Grable, Ann Miller, Don Ameche were all regulars…What must it have been like?

We arrived at the track Saturday morning. Licensing went smoothly, and after meeting with Jack's trainer, we headed back to our hotel to get ready for the races. By the time we returned, people were already thronging in. There was valet parking for the jockeys, which was a first for us, and Jack, suited up, sunglasses on, and wheeling in his jockey's bag with his whips protruding, was getting looks from some of the many pretty girls. His mind was on the job at hand, however, and after a quick "good luck," he was into the jockeys room.

For me, then, I had the prospect of a long afternoon at the Del Mar races, which suited me just fine. Until I discovered the ten dollar beer. Now, I am feckless where money is concerned, I am afraid. It just runs through my fingers. But even I took a deep breath when, after receiving a half pint of draft beer in a plastic cup, I was charged ten dollars—and don't forget the tip! That's twenty dollars per pint, plus obligatory few dollars' tip. That's around sixteen pounds in our old English money. For which you could probably escape a conviction for assault on a bartender back home.

This ordinarily would not have been much of a problem; I do not usually drink much at the races, two drinks would have done me, and all I would have is this anecdote.

It was not to be however. I have a cousin in Los Angeles; he is involved in the television industry. He was working, but when I contacted him he said an editor friend of his was going to be there, and he took my number and we arranged to meet up.

And so, after a couple races and a bit of searching, I met up with Chester and his seven-year-old son, Tristan. It turned out that Chester had gone to college in San Diego and grown to love carefree days out at Del Mar racetrack. He was in town for a few days' holiday to relax and have fun…and his wife wasn't at the races with him. Well, I think you can guess what happened next.

Beer after beer was drunk, bet after bet was placed, fun was had. And before we knew it, Jack's first race was upon us.

It was great to see him walk out there into the paddock and ride out on the horse through the walkway, and out onto the track for the post parade. Beautiful horses watched by beautiful people, with the sun shining and the palm trees towering high against the terracotta grandstand, all of it set against the backdrop of the Pacific Ocean. This was the sport as it was supposed to be.

Taylor Lane, the first runner, broke well, and Jack slotted her in a perfect position on the rail. The race was a mile on the turf around two turns. He sat quiet, waiting. Around the last bend, a gap appeared, and he moved her up, gaining lengths, and as they fanned into the straight with the crowd roaring, he pulled her out to challenge, into fourth, and then into third. She was 30/1, and there was only a furlong left to run… But then she tired a little, and her stride faltered, and other runners passed her late. He had given her a great ride, though, and she had shown up well for the owners. The second runner didn't bring his best game, but they went around fine, and when I met Jack on his way back to the jocks room to introduce him to Chester and Tristan, he was in great form.

After he washed and changed, he came out and met us, and we watched the last couple of races together, so he could soak up the atmosphere. I looked at him in his suit; he fitted right in here, with his blond hair and blue eyes, and I thought about how far he had come in such a short time. Still only eighteen, with fifty-six winners already under his belt, and now he'd just ridden against Gary Stevens and Mike Smith at one of the most famous and glamorous race meets in the world five thousand miles from his hometown of Newmarket. And I thought about how proud I was of him. And then he looked at me. His father. Standing there beside him. And he said, "Are you drunk?"

On Sunday, we awoke with a rare free day. We headed down to the track once more, saw a few people, watched a few races, and Jack collected his riding gear. Then we drove back along the coastal road, with the sun shining down on us, and the Pacific glistening to the right of us, and beautiful people in Mercedes and Ferraris in front and behind us. And Jack, with his dad, in a minivan.

When we got back to the hotel, we changed into our trunks and headed for the sea.

We laughed more together messing about in the ocean, the waves half knocking us over, than we had in a long time. Our experience in the States has mostly been very good and often been great. But it has also been hard and tough and worrisome and frightening. Jack has done well riding, but we know mistakes were made in how we did things, and he could have done much better, and that has made me feel bad, and sad sometimes. So that morning on the beach, just larking about, in and out of the Pacific Ocean, was a chance for us to just be us, no horses, no racing. Just the sea and sand and sunshine. Me and my boy. And in spite of Vicky warning me, I forgot to go and get us sunscreen, and we are still peeling now, two weeks later. It was great.

Chapter 31

The Bug Year: August 2015

Ellis Park, Indiana Grand

The heat and the driving continued, and for Jack, the work and the dieting continued. But the winners weren't coming. Nothing even looked like it might win. Day after day, ride after ride. Week after week. He was hungry, painfully thin, tired. He took the lack of winners better than me. He took everything better than me. But I was there, all the time, watching, worrying, getting stressed. No help, of course, but there you are. It's harder when it's out of your hands.

There may be places I would rather be less in the middle of a blazing hot summer than Ellis Park or Indiana Grand. But off the top of my head, I cannot think of any. Ellis Park was a

201

four-hundred-mile round trip from Lexington, and Indiana three hundred and fifty, and there is a lesser known theory of relativity that applies only to racing people, that Einstein seems to have missed: It states that the distance and time taken to get home from any racetrack is halved after a winner and doubled without one. And that is true, you know.

It was four weeks, fifty-seven rides, six thousand five hundred miles driven, making twenty-one fruitless trips to the races, before the drought broke. The month was nearly out; it was the twenty-third of August, and all Jack had to show for it was a solitary second place in a cheap claiming race.

Then, that Sunday at Ellis Park, he landed two wins in consecutive races. That's how it goes. Up and down… She's Lying Again and Barnyard Fiddler were the fun-named racers, both trained by the same small stable, which made it a big deal for them too.

During the day, the track held some novelty dog racing. The little Dachshunds owners' would stand by the winning post, facing down the track toward the miniature starting gates, ready to call their tiny mutts to them, and the first one to reach its owner was the winner. The crowd would fall silent, and the commentator would shout, "They're off!" And the gates would spring open. And all hell would break loose! It was hilarious chaos. Half of the dogs would execute a sharp right or left turn immediately leaving the gate, bumping into and knocking over their opponents; some would get excited and jump on a fellow dog ruining both their chances; and there was usually at least one who would attack the small number cloth tied around its belly and roll around on the ground wrestling it off. Eventually, with the crowd in fits of laughter, one saintly pup would run up and greet its owner, tail wagging, and be declared the victor. Jack said every rider in the room would watch the mayhem, laughing and cheering them home. They really are the best fun.

Ellis also brings in petting animals; I think I saw a llama there—but it could just have been the heat. And I believe they have also held ostrich races, with the jockeys actually riding them… We suggested Jack give that one a miss.

All these entertainments were well received by the crowd, and I really do think some diversification could pay dividends for horse racing in North America. Americans love a day out; they enjoy their leisure time and embrace new experiences. So small novelties to lighten a day at the races, I think, could make the whole experience more family friendly, and I think for the future health of the sport, families and college kids need to be a key target audience.

You can have a drink and eat and gamble at the races. If your children could have pony rides and visit the petting zoo, and if there were fun distractions like novelty dog racing, then I think it could help the perception of the sport here. In Europe, a trip to the races is a family day out. It could be here too, I think, and it is important that it is. Because it is as a kid that you can become hooked on the sport, on the horses, on the whole thing.

Three days later, Jack won a nice maiden race at Indiana Grand, and two days after that, back at Ellis, he made it win number four for the month. All of them had come within a space of five days, and they, just about, saved the month. But it wasn't what we wanted; it wasn't the way we wanted his bug to end. With just one full month of Jack's apprenticeship left, his light was shining a little dimly. It had been a decent year really, but there just hadn't been anything to mark him out, to make people remember him. Nothing to stop him sinking without a trace when his weight allowance had gone, and he had to ride at level weights against the seniors.

There was, though, one other noteworthy event for the month. It was when Jack was booked to ride Emma Spencer. This caused a bit of mirth in our house. I presume that the equine Emma Spencer was named after the stylish English racing presenter of the same name, and when word got out, there was plenty of childish leg-pulling and immature innuendo from his friends back home in Newmarket, which I tried to dampen. So, after he had ridden her, I approached him, and asked him what he thought. "She made a bit of a noise," he replied. "Well done." I said.

August total: 4 wins from 62 rides
Bug Year total: 57 wins from 608 ride

Chapter 32

Emigration

Not many people ever emigrate. And most people who do tend to move from a poorer country to a wealthier one. Not me.

In 1970, at the age of five, I boarded a plane with my mother, elder sister, and younger brother. She was escaping a husband who had a drink problem. He wasn't really a bad man, I don't think. But he did some bad things when he was drunk.

She did the right thing for all of us, my mother. But I still feel bad sometimes to think what a shock it must have been for my father when he came home from work one day, and his whole family had left him.

We flew from JFK in New York to London's Heathrow airport. In one day, I went from living in by far the wealthiest, most advanced country in the world to inhabiting one that, although civilized and decent, was, at that time, a poorer, duller, damper, and more parochial vision of the Western world than I knew.

Things like ice cubes were luxury items. Warm soda and cold bedrooms were the norm. At times in the 1970s, bread in the supermarkets and electricity in your home seemed to be luxuries that were hard to come by.

But I was just a young kid and took it in my stride—except when the fog came down, which would leave me bedridden and unable to breathe or literally stride anywhere.

I remember evening tea in the black midwinter, cosy in my grandmother's council-owned flat in Balham, South London. Warm yellow lamplight in the kitchen, the cute little German weather vane clock with tiny figures in traditional garb, that would be in or out depending on the weather (mostly in). A pot of tea, raisin toast, the radio on. A different age.

She had nothing really, my grandmother, but she was quietly dignified. She reminded me of an Irish version of the Queen, quietly doing her duty, imperturbable. She had lived in London during the Blitz and blamed Adolf Hitler for her only vice, a solitary cigarette each Christmas Day.

With the help of her son, she bought that council flat years later in the 1980s, when then Prime Minister Margaret Thatcher brought in a right to buy at discounted prices for tenants in government-owned housing. That modest flat would almost have made her a property millionaire now, were she still alive. I wonder what she would have said, if someone had told her that when she was working in a local cardboard-box factory all those years ago, modestly getting by each week.

And I wonder also whether such a scheme, which brought millions of citizens in the United Kingdom up from the ranks of the working-class renting poor into middle class homeowners, could be used to help the working poor here in America, many of whom are African American and descended from the involuntary immigrants brought here hundreds of years ago and forced to work against their will, for no pay, to help create the wealth of America, and yet to never get to share in it. I don't know about you, but I would be angry if that happened to me. Maybe something like that could help a bit, make amends a bit. Make people who maybe often feel excluded to feel more included, more enfranchised, more hopeful about their situation.

I grew up as a kid, firstly, in South London, and then out to Banstead, near Epsom in Surrey, which was where I discovered and grew to love horses, and soon after, horse racing. So, NASA's loss was to become the British horse racing industry's gain, as I slowly abandoned my ambition to become the world's first asthmatic astronaut and opted instead to become the world's first jockey with broken-wind.

For some reason though, through all those years, I kept my American identity. Now, I know that if I had happened to have been born in a stable, that wouldn't have made me a horse. So, my Irish ancestry probably made me more Irish than American. And I had lived in the United States for only the first five and a bit years of my life, and then spent the next forty years in England.

But I had no English ancestry, and although the UK tolerates immigrants very well, they do not integrate and assimilate them as they do in America. I think most second-generation immigrants in the States would identify themselves as American first, followed by their ancestral heritage. In Britain, that would normally be the other way around. That's not a criticism, just an observation.

England was a good country to grow up in, and my asthma wasn't a financial burden to my family thanks to the National Health Service, one of the most humane and civilized institutions ever created. And I think Britain is like the NHS, really, it is reflected in it. Maybe there isn't enough money to go around, maybe things are stretched, maybe it could be friendlier or cleaner. Maybe it could be better. But it is civilized, it is decent, and it tries not to leave anyone behind, not the poor, not the vulnerable, not the failures, not the old, not the weak. It may not always succeed, but the intentions are good. It may be old and a bit tired, a bit jaded, sometimes a bit ugly in places. But it is venerable, it is esteemed, it is a model other countries aspired to, and many copied. It led the world when it was younger, but it is not young now. Now, it is getting older.

Today, there are other younger countries who shape the world. And of course, for most of the last hundred years, the baton has been passed to the USA. A country built around an idea, around a philosophy of how to live, of how to be, of what civilization and the human race could and should be.

The American Declaration of Independence, published on the Fourth of July 1776, was a beautifully and articulately written fuck-off letter to King George III of England. It basically stated that the reason the colonists all got on a ship and undertook a dangerous voyage to a wild, untamed land was to get away from the robbery and tyranny of the rich and powerful against the poor and religiously oppressed of Europe. And they weren't going to stand for the same thing happening here. It also gave voice to its authors' famous set of ideals for the American colonies, declaring that all men are created equal, and all men should have the right to pursue life, liberty, and happiness as free men.

This was a revolutionary idea. So revolutionary, in fact, that it started a war. The colonists won. And the United States of America was born. A country created by immigrants, for immigrants. A nation united not by a race or shared history, but by a set of ideals. It was, and remains for many, a utopia, or as close to one as mere humans could hope to create.

And it worked. In less than two hundred years, North America was transformed from a huge wilderness into the most advanced developed nation on Earth.

The Founding Fathers, however, apparently didn't see the irony in creating America to escape oppression themselves, by then oppressing and enslaving Africans and dispossessing and eradicating the Native Americans. I suppose the boot was on the other foot.

In spite of these huge sins, the United States of America has been seen by much of the world as a beacon, a light of freedom, and equality, and progress. And a country that stood up for its beliefs, and for its friends and allies. It became technologically, militarily, and financially the most powerful nation on earth. Ever.

And yes, it had resources, it was mineral rich, oil rich, fertile. It was abundant, and the resources were exploited with an energy never seen before. It was the energy of capitalism, of free men unshackled by custom, by birth, by class. The rewards went to the hungriest, the smartest, the most ambitious. And the most ruthless also, of course.

And it may not have been perfect, but it was the best there had ever been. If you were born white and American in the late 1960s you had won the lottery of life. And I was, and I had. And my mother threw away my ticket...

So, over the years, when misfortune struck, when things didn't go my way, when hard times came, and progress hit a brick wall, I would often think about America, and wonder whether I would have got on better there. Whether England, with its class system wasn't where I should be.

Newmarket and Newmarket heath, is a place of haves and have not's. Lords and knights in cars, driving by immigrants on bicycles. So, especially in the early days, I felt a bit like I shouldn't be there. I felt a bit of an imposter. I didn't really acknowledge all this when I set out, I just felt it. I felt like someone was about to shout out, "Hoi! What do you think you are doing here?"

But the truth is, my fellow trainers were, almost to a man, most polite and welcoming, and in the end, I spent twenty years living and training in Newmarket, I suppose, in the end, I became a small part of the racing furniture found there. I went there almost straight after I finished my equine degree in Warwickshire, where I met my English, very middle-class, wife-to-be.

I started well; I was lucky enough to have a good horse early, and I got more than my fair share of coverage thanks to him. But the bigger owners never came. So, I got a bit jaded, a bit disillusioned.

And I talked about America, there, like an itch I had never scratched. And I filled my son's head with how great things were there, how Newmarket was a town so full of hard luck stories, but America was still a land of opportunity. And he visited Kentucky's racing academy on an exchange visit, and legendary retired jockey Chris McCarron was its director, and he took Jack and his friend Ben around and showed them North American racing, and they loved it. And Jack came home with a dream of returning one day as a jockey.

After he finished school, he spent a year working for Sir Mark Prescott. And after he had ridden four winners, somehow, thanks to Vicky's diligence, she and Jack got green cards through me. And I found myself emigrating for the second time in my life. Back to America.

But it was harder the second time. And I was probably too old really, at forty-eight, to emigrate really successfully. I think you need to be younger, to have more of your productive working life in front of you, than behind. I had too many roots put down in England, and they ran too deep by now. It was hard for Vicky too, but Jack settled in quickly, and within a week of landing in New York was exercising horses in Kentucky, and a few weeks after that he was riding his first race stateside.

He hasn't really stopped since. He has some money in the bank, a couple of cars, and a career still hopefully going on and up. He is living the American Dream. But he has to work hard for it. We have driven the equivalent of six times around the circumference of the Earth since we have been here, travelling to training tracks in the mornings and races in the afternoons and evenings. He eats half what every other young man eats, and that is tough in a country like this. He doesn't smoke, doesn't drink, is in the gym every day. And he is riding highly strung Thoroughbreds at speed morning, noon, and sometimes night, day in, day out. He is living the American dream because he has toughed it out.

But that is the thing. I have seen young riders in England working just as hard, making as many sacrifices, but all to no avail. The opportunities just didn't come for them. And I see them years later, in the pubs, enjoying a drink, working in the stables, getting by, letting their great dreams go, replacing them with small pleasures. And to be honest, without knowing it, for many it is a blessing in disguise. Because success brings its own pressures, and whilst earning good money is nice, as long as you can pay your bills, you are as happy, in your own way, as a richer man.

Sometimes you may be in the stands watching a sportsman or an actor or a singer and wish you could be them. But they are working while you watch them on a weekend. You are there with a beer and a hot dog. You are relaxed; they are tense. You won't be in the news if you foul up personally or at work; they will be.

And to do all this as an immigrant is doubly tough. To be away from your friends, away from your family, away from everything you used to be. It is okay when everything is going well. But everything is never going well all the time for anyone, especially in horseracing, which is a roller coaster of a life.

So, we didn't come to America because it was easy; we didn't come here to goof off, or to make excuses, or take it easy. We came here because we felt, we thought, we desperately hoped, that our lives—our son's life—could be better if we emigrated.

And that is why people emigrate. People who emigrate are dreaming, are hoping, are choosing optimism over despair, or defeat, or resigned acceptance of their lot. And sometimes people are emigrating now, just to try to save their lives, their children's lives.

Emigrating isn't easy. You leave your home behind, your family behind, your friends. All you knew, all you were is gone, all your history. People trade all that for hope. It is hard, and it is scary, and it takes a lot from you. But people who are prepared to endure all that should be embraced because they are the adventurers, the can-do's, the never-be-beatens.

And that is the spirit of America. It is still the spirit of the immigrant.

Chapter 33

Hit and Run

I suppose there comes a time in many people's lives, especially when they have passed the first flush of youth, that they experience a moment of clarity, a moment when they think, *Is this how I thought I would end up? Is this what I have come to?*

Those are questions that tend to come to me when I am perching—not sitting—with thigh muscles straining, over a toilet facility at a service station, in the middle of nowhere in Middle America, a hundred or more miles from where we currently reside, and thousands of miles from where I lived nearly all my life, while trying to squeeze one out.

You see, I think we can all agree that the older one gets, the more one likes to have the sanctuary of their own en-suite. It is a comfort, it is yours, and any strange smells are yours too, and that is important. And it is clean, and quiet, and no one is going to try to open the door, or start banging on it at an inopportune moment. And there is toilet paper, and it is soft and luxuriant, and if you run out you can shout, real loud, and more will be delivered to you. So, I cannot tell you how hard it has been, how uncomfortable, how distressing—for all concerned—to find myself away from home, day after day, when nature calls.

During Jack's bug year, we covered over seventy thousand miles up and down and across the highways of America. And due to my fondness for coffee and spicy food, our trips have often been marred by the sudden development of an urgent—if not emergency—situation.

In our family, this grave scenario has been labelled the Hit and Run. To surmise: when the need arises, we speed onward to the nearest possible facility with such conveniences. I hit it. Then we run.

It may, I suppose, sound mildly amusing to some. But the truth is, there, under the hot summer sun in this alien land, seeking something, yet being scared of what you might find as you open that cubicle door, what dilemma you may be left with, what dire straits you may find yourself in, well, it's not funny at all. For a middle-aged man to face this challenge several times a week is beyond a trial. It is a form of torture designed to strip from oneself any last shred of dignity that life to date had not already taken.

But if you cannot grow wiser with age, then you are a fool indeed. And so, whilst I didn't go so far as to create a database,

I did begin to make mental notes of each place the deed was done. I began to grade them, to rate them, to compare them. And what I found, of course, is that not all facilities are equal. And whilst there is certainly no place like home where this job is concerned, there are some places I have encountered where, if the urge hits me, I can proceed with a tranquil state of mind, soothed by the prospect of a civilized experience. While there are other places, so awful that once encountered the sheer horror of the experience can never be erased from your mind.

And so, in a spirit of solidarity with my fellow traveller, I am going to share here my reviews of the restrooms I have encountered in my recent journeys around the States. Please think of this as the first Michelin-style guide to public restroom facilities. I think it is long overdue.

Starbucks. Civilized, clean, spacious. Surprisingly nice décor. Stay awhile.

McDonald's. Very disappointing compared to similar restaurants in the UK, where it is famous for its cleanliness. Okay in emergency situations, but otherwise best avoided.

Keeneland. Worth saving one up specially. Almost better than being at home. A refuge from the madness of the world, with state-of-the-art superpowered flushing.

Turfway Park. Unusable. Dirty, smelly, in poor repair, and poorly monitored. A prison style facility.

Ellis Park. Never. Ever. Do not even think about it. Unusable. I swear I saw urine dripping from the ceiling once. A skunk would hold its nose. The Pee Patch.

Service stations. Too many to count. Generally avoid like the plague—which you may contract if you visit one. To be fair, some are tolerable. But some are like a coprologists trophy room, and you don't know which until you're inside. Are you feeling lucky punk? Well, are you?

Belterra Park. Casino facilities quite nice; racetrack facilities, no.

Indiana Grand. Possibly the best thing about the place.

Churchill Downs. Fourth floor and above, highly recommended (see Keeneland). Lower floors, only in emergency, bring your own tissue.

Kentucky Downs. Casino fine. Otherwise it's an outhouse. No, really. It is an outhouse.

Mahoning Valley. Fine, but not worth the journey.

Panera Bread. Okay. But they look at you rudely on your way out, so maybe buy something. Some people…

Mountaineer. Hotel and casino okay. Wasn't man enough to check out the racetrack.

Del Mar. Couldn't perform. Think it was the flight.

I hope this is of some help to you, should the situation ever arise.

(Note to editor: You have missed an S from the start of the chapter title).

Chapter 34

The Bug Year: September 2015

Indiana Grand, Ellis Park,
Kentucky Downs, Churchill Downs

Jack was heading into the last full month of his bug. It looked like he was going to get a week or so extension due to time off for injuries, but he was well inside the final furlong now.

With fifty-seven winners on the board, the obvious target was to get past sixty wins. He was desperate to get past one million in purse money won by his mounts for the calendar year too, but that looked a big ask, as his mounts would have to pick up nearly four hundred thousand dollars in the next four weeks—the previous month his mounts had not even earned fifty thousand.

It started well enough, though, with a minor win and a second on the fifth of the month at Ellis Park, as it was closing out its meet. He picked up a couple more seconds there the following week, so his total was fifty-eight wins by the time he moved his tack back up to Churchill Downs for their short September meet.

Three seconds and a few minor places put about twenty thousand into the prize pool on the first few days racing there, but there were no wins. A couple of days racing at Indiana Grand followed, and then it was time for Kentucky Downs' annual five-day meet.

Kentucky Downs is a European style turf track located in southwest Kentucky, close to the Tennessee border, about one hundred and sixty miles from Lexington. It is a casino track, and the slice of the pie to support purse money it diverts from the year-round slot profits is all poured into those five short days of racing. It means maiden races run for one hundred and thirty thousand dollars, and average prize money per day is well north of a million dollars. It is a good place to have a winner!

Jack only had nine rides over the five days, and it was always going to be a tough call, as, with the big prize money on offer, the top riders were keen to get as many mounts as possible. But European riders have a good record there, unsurprisingly, being quite at home on the undulating turf track. Jack liked it, and he struck—at 60/1, in a four-horse photo, by a head, a neck, and a head against a who's who of top North American riders.

In one fell swoop, he put his name back out there again, winning a $130,000 allowance in a tight finish against the big name riders, and he added nearly fifty thousand to his purse money total. *Just one more,* we thought, *make it sixty.* That's good here, for a bug riding Churchill and Keeneland.

He did it in style in the end. Another close finish, back at Churchill. A minor race, but an important one for Jack, and we were pleased it came at Churchill Downs. Win number sixty!

And then the following week, he struck there again in another valuable allowance race on the turf. He stole it from the front, setting slow early fractions and blazing home in hot pink silks at 32/1. Another $50,000 race. And with that win really, finally, he had earned his stripes. Trainers were acknowledging him that hadn't before, greeting him by name, accepting him. It had taken time, but he had got there, in the nick of time, by the skin of his teeth, before his bug boy status disappeared, he had become an accepted part of the elite Kentucky riding colony.

He managed to bag one more victory before the month was out, a minor race at Indiana on a cold wet day, but a storming, determined ride.

So, it was nearly done now. The fat lady was about to sing. But there was one goal left, one thing that would really be the dream ending. He had two weeks of bug left, and his tack was on its way to Keeneland. Just one win there, that would be the dream finish.

Just one more win.

September total: 5 wins 77 rides
Bug Year total: 62 wins 685 rides

Chapter 35

American Racehorse

It was at Keeneland that I first got to know the American Thoroughbred. The "dirt" horse. It was there, for the first time, that I saw many of them together, up close. The really good ones. And I thought they were magnificent.

They are bigger than a typical European turf horse. Stronger, deeper, lower. Broader chests, stronger shoulders, more angular, slightly longer backed. The European Thoroughbred is a composition of circles, the American dirt horse is a medley of triangles.

And they walk differently. The European grass horse is a ballet dancer. Spring heeled, nimble. Dancing and coiled and skittish. The dirt horse walks deliberately, slowly, heavily. Its head low, purposeful, without rushing. Like a gunslinger.

223

The European turf horse is beautiful like summer in the English countryside. The American dirthorse is beautiful like a thunderstorm coming over the Rocky Mountains.

Horseracing has a surprisingly long history in the New World. It was way back in 1664 that English colonel Richard Nicolls sailed four British frigates into New Amsterdam and anchored them just off, what is now, Brooklyn. The Dutch colonists who had set up there were hopelessly outmanned and outgunned, and peacefully surrendered their territory to the British, who promptly renamed the settlement New York.

Colonel Nicolls seemed to have been a popular enough leader, and he was an ardent fan of horse racing. He arranged for a racecourse to be laid out on the turf at what is now known as Hempstead Plain, in Nassau County, and offered a silver cup to be raced for twice a year. He named his new racecourse Newmarket. It was the first racecourse in North America.

Over the centuries that followed, racing grew widely popular, and seemingly most places colonists went, so did horse racing. And as the crowds of spectators grew, some courses configured themselves into ovals, so the races could be viewed more easily, and then some courses "skinned" the tracks by removing the top layer of turf, so producing faster times. And the American love of speed and dirt was born. And a different type of horse flourished in these conditions.

The American Thoroughbred derives its Arab blood from imported European stock. Diomed, the winner of the very first running of the Epsom Derby, was an early imported stallion, and he, together with other immigrant stock began shaping the breed in the newly formed United States. So, stallions and mares arrived, and they were bred with stock already here. And eventually, over the decades and centuries that followed, some of these American racehorses were exported to Europe, and some of them did well. Back and forth, back and forth. What busy bees we are.

And now Thoroughbreds are exported from the United States to race all over the world, desired for their speed and toughness.

Over twenty thousand mostly dirt-bred Thoroughbreds were produced in America last year. A lot of horses. But only half of what was produced twenty-five years earlier. Racing in North America isn't thriving as it once was. It isn't often in the public's mind anymore. The racegoers are getting older, and the younger generation don't seem to be engaging with it. The sport has lost its sparkle in North America, lost public interest. The facilities are not always what they should be for a modern sporting event. The TV signals are sometimes poor quality. It needs new ideas. It needs strong governance. It needs marketing. The drugs issue has turned people off. And so has the dirt. Horses get hurt more on dirt. And riders. People don't like that. I don't like that.

We are in the twenty-first century, but American horse racing sometimes seems like it is not. Somehow, it got left behind. It fell behind. It got a bit lost somewhere along the way, over time. North America permitted the use of painkillers

225

and Lasix in a bid to keep horses racing, and so maintain field sizes. Field sizes have declined ever since, as have starts per horse per year. Dirt racing was an early nineteenth century innovation. What would the NFL be today, I wonder, if the players still wore those old breeches and leather helmets, and used a pigskin football that could only be thrown half the distance of today's ball? What if their grandstands were old and rusty? And the televised pictures grainy and every camera angle the same old shot?

The NFL looks shiny and new, like a twenty something, ready to make their mark on the world. Stateside racing sometimes seems like an old man, seeing out his days, half ignored, half looked after. Not looking forward, just set in his ways.

So, Keeneland is an inspiration - and nobody does the big occasions as well as Americans; like the Triple Crown and Breeders Cup. And I am sure Saratoga must be wonderful. But, away from these special occasions, on the whole, day to day, the sport is maybe not what it could be. North American racing has done a great job in creating and sustaining funding for their sport, and I personally think (and I did spend a year doing nothing but visiting racetracks here – so I think I get some say) it would be good to invest a bit of that money in the facilities at the smaller tracks. It wouldn't be too massive a task I think for them to be clean, and freshly painted, and for the food to be better. A good burger really isn't that much harder or more expensive to make than a bad one. And I think all that would make for a better race-going experience for fans – and fans to be.

But the biggest thing I think, holding racing in North America back, is safety. I think, as long as safety of the competitors is taking a backseat, that American racing will probably never amount to much more than a fringe activity here again. That's a shame really isn't it, when you think about it? Dirt increases risk of catastrophic injury. States with more permissive medication rules have more fatal racetrack accidents. Toe grabs and turndowns on the horses shoes are dangerous and unnecessary, and can cause horrific accidents when horses clip heels. Two out of three of those issues could be fixed overnight couldn't they, if people cared enough? When I think about all the horses and brave riders hurt, and worse, unnecessarily, it makes me angry. If anyone ever wants to discuss this with me, I would be very pleased to accommodate them. It's easy enough to find me. I'm the twitchy one down on the track apron come post time.

And so, although Jack loves it all here, and there is a lot that I love about it too. I sometimes find it tough to fully embrace the sport here, as it is. Please forgive me, as I have a selfish interest, but I am torn when comparing dirt racing to the turf. It is thunderous and thrilling. But it is sometimes too ugly and brutish.

The competitors themselves though. The American Racehorse. I can embrace them. They are very beautiful to perceive.

Chapter 36

The Dueling Grounds

What a name! Evocative, dangerous, romantic, illicit. But not, as far as the racecourse is concerned, very historic.

The Dueling Grounds in Franklin, Kentucky, was a 260-acre plot of land sat right next to the Tennessee border. In the eighteenth and early nineteenth century, duelling was illegal in Tennessee, but not in Kentucky. So, when two gentlemen had a difference to be addressed, they would arrange to meet on this piece of land and settle their grudge the old-fashioned way.

By the mid-nineteenth century, duelling was outlawed in Kentucky too, and although this seemingly did nothing to dim Americans' enthusiasm for shooting one another (40,000 last year), it did mean that there was a patch of land on the

Kentucky-Tennessee border which was now redundant. For the next 150 years or so, the land was farmed, until, in the late 1980s, a group of investors thought that, with its proximity to Nashville, it could be a good spot for a racetrack.

The track they created was, and still is, unique in North America. A European style, left-hand, undulating, mile and a quarter, turf-only course. The first meet took place as recently as 1990 and was steeplechase only. In 1998 the track was—in my opinion, disappointingly—renamed Kentucky Downs, and in 2007, a new group of investors took a majority interest in the facility.

Today Kentucky Downs offers only five days of flat racing each September—and 364 days a year of casino-style slots. Sorry. I meant, "historic racing."

"Historic racing," or "instant racing," is the biggest wheeze I have come across in a long, long, time. Ever, in fact. The casino-style racetrack, where racecourses are granted a licence to build casinos with a stipulation that part of the profits are put toward purse money for the horse racing, have often been successful. They create, on the whole, pretty soulless racetracks (Belterra Park is an exception) that do offer good purses for the racing (Belterra Park is an exception here too) and so help provide many horsemen with a decent living.

The commonwealth of Kentucky, however, has refused to legalize any casinos within its borders, for, as far as I can gather, mostly ethical reasons. And as a result, the state with the greatest racing heritage and the source of the best Thoroughbreds in North America has at times found itself struggling to compete purse-wise with some of its neighbours.

Now, I don't know who came up with the idea of "historic racing," but I doff my cap to them, for they must possess the cunning of a fox and the chutzpah of Phineas Barnum himself.

A historic-racing machine looks like a slot machine. You press the same buttons as a slot machine. And cherries and bells spin around like a slot machine. And if they align, the machine chirps and bleeps and flashes and rewards you with money, like a slot machine. But apparently, it isn't a slot machine. It's a bit like someone offering to sell you a horse by describing it as a historic car. "Really?" you say doubt-fully. "It sure looks like a horse..." "Oh no no, my friend! You misunderstand! Do you not see that horn I have placed between its ears? And the car seat upon its back?"

So yes, if you look very carefully, low down on each machine you will find a TV screen a few inches square, and with each press of the play button, a replay of the last few seconds of an archive race is shown, and somehow, appar-ently, that is related to the cherries and bells that come up, and all the machines are linked so the money is pooled as a pari-mutuel wager and paid out on the same basis to those who have aligned their bells and cherries. And as a pari-mutuel machine, it is legal, allegedly, and therefore not outlawed in the commonwealth of Kentucky.

It is a hilarious fudge; no European Union bureaucrat could have come up with a more ingenious circumnavigation of the stated legislation.

One thing is for sure, though. At Kentucky Downs, these are money-making machines of Warren Buffett proportions. There are around six hundred units installed in the casino at Kentucky Downs—which quite frankly, is in the exact middle of nowhere—and they are currently raking in around fifty million dollars. That's per month, by the way. Month in, month out...

So, what all that casino revenue translates to is this: Little Kentucky Downs. Here in Franklin, Kentucky, in a very rural, very tranquil, very sparsely populated part of the country. On a racetrack marked out around a field by white railings, with no grandstand and only five days of racing a year. They offer the highest average daily purses of any meet in all of North America. Their five days of racing offer total prize money just shy of eight million dollars. Maiden races run here for $130,000, and the Kentucky Turf Cup, a Grade 3 event run over a mile and a half, offers a total purse of $600,000. This means the top jockeys fly in, and the top trainers send their horses, and fields are full, and betting handle is around $4,000,000 a day. Which makes me wonder if, possibly, a relentless diet of oval dirt races needn't be the be all and end all of North American racing, after all—a view which is perhaps supported by the fact Kentucky Downs was recently voted number one track by the Horseplayers Association of North America.

I think it's a great place. Basic maybe, but pleasant and fun. And, after Keeneland, it is the next racetrack I would take a newcomer to racing in Kentucky to show them a good time. The people who work here are enthusiastic and seem like they are having fun too, and you can tell people care about this place and are proud of what they have produced, and they seem genuinely pleased to see you.

The commentators are great, they sound excited about the races, and they impart a lot of information. Horse racing is a unique sporting occasion in the sense that there are only a couple of minutes of action every half an hour. That is a great opportunity to entertain and inform your customers, and to make fans out of first-timers. Pre- and post-race interviews with jockeys and trainers would be a welcome addition at tracks stateside, I think.

And, if I thought the commentators loved their jobs, that was nothing compared to the people manning the grill where I went to get one of their very good burgers. When I went back a year later, the guy serving remembered me! (I suppose that could be saying something about me, now I think about it.) So, you can sit on the chairs provided out in the sun, next to the rail, and watch the horses go by, while eating your food and enjoying a beer or a soda and listening to the commentators' jabber on, and it is really pleasant. Really nice. And like something from yesteryear. Simple, but satisfying.

When it comes to the actual races, European riders do well here. Leading jockey Florent Geroux could probably make a nice living just riding these five days and taking the rest of the year off. And Jack was keen to try to get a slice of this lucrative pie.

The first day he just had the one mount, but on the second day he had four booked, and one of them we thought might have a shot at the money. Ubiquitous Mantle was her name. A four-year-old filly who began her career in Ireland. She had won at Leopardstown racecourse over there, so we knew an undulating track would hold no fears for her. And when we reviewed her races, we thought perhaps this was a filly who did not take kindly to the whip. Some horses don't. Eclipse, the unbeaten champion racehorse and leading sire of the eighteenth century in England, from whom around ninety-five percent of modern Thoroughbreds can trace their tail male lineage back to, it was said, "would not run for whip nor spur."

The filly was trained by the androgynously named Michael Ann Ewing, a petite but formidable lady, full of fun and energy. She and Jack had formed a very successful partnership. He trusted her and her team implicitly, and he knew Michael liked the filly.

She was entered for a $130,000 allowance. They don't give away that sort of money, and after an initial promising debut stateside, her form had disappointed a little, so she was 60/1 in the betting. But this was to be her first start since being under the care of Michael. And Jack didn't think she was that much of a longshot.

Her lime green silks were easy to pick out in the race. There is a right-handed dogleg, just after the mile start, and when we walked the track and discussed it, Jack said he would take a hard right to there, before re-joining the field as they entered the left-hand home turn. And that was just what he did; the only one to go with him was top European rider Kieren Fallon, who stayed upside him on his outer. Jack switched left at just the right time, and the pair of them dropped down on the field and hit the entrance to the home turn in first and second, respectively.

The filly was still travelling nicely as they began to exit the turn and straighten up for the roughly three furlong, slightly uphill finish—longer and more testing than most finishing stretches in the States. Kieren's filly quickly cried enough, and the field was closing around Jack. When he asked her, though, she found, she stretched, and she fought to hold her lead, like some good fillies do. One after another they challenged her up the straight—which seemed to be getting longer by the second! But she kept repelling them. Jack waved his stick but refrained from using it, even as two joined either side of him, even when he could taste that winning post. And in the last twenty yards, he put both hands on the reins and pushed for what he was worth as a splash of pink emerged from nowhere and flashed past him as they crossed the line.

It was too close to call. Jack didn't know. He said Corey Lanerie, the rider in pink, might have known, because he shouted something that rhymes with luck as they shot past the post. But it was very tight, and the result took a long time to come.

"First, number eight," called the judge, "Ubiquitous Mantle."

They had their picture taken in the winner's circle, and the commentator talked about nineteen-year-old Jack Gilligan from Newmarket scoring his first win at Kentucky Downs. And the boy was happy as a lark walking back into the jocks room.

Once inside, he took off his helmet and body protector and silks, and he sat down on the bench to sip some water. "Bad luck, Jack," said the young California-born, Kentucky-based rider Chris Landeros, who was sitting opposite him.

"What do you mean?" Jack replied, a bit concerned.

"Well, she's Irish bred," said Chris. Jack picked up the program book. Fully half of the prize money for the race was available only if the horse had been bred in Kentucky, which meant Jack's win percentage had just dropped from an expected $7,800 to around $3,800. Now, don't get me wrong, $4,000 is a nice day's work. Unless, that is, you were expecting $8,000.

Understandably his mood was a bit dampened by the end of the day when he got back in the car for the journey home. As we pulled onto the highway, he asked me, "Did you back it?"

"No," I admitted. He shot me a look of ill-concealed disgust.

It is one hundred and seventy miles back to Lexington from Kentucky Downs. It was a surprisingly quiet journey home that evening. Both of us lost in thoughts of what could have been.

Chapter 37

October

Keeneland, Indiana Grand

A couple of higher profile wins in September had kept business brisk. On the first day of the month, Jack rode at Indiana Grand, and two days later rode one on the first day of the autumn meet at Keeneland, followed by a mad dash up to ride that same evening at Indiana. The next day he rode a few at Keeneland, but between them there wasn't a winner.

Two days later, on Tuesday the sixth, he was back up at Indiana, and again drew a blank. The rest of the month, though, was Keeneland, which suited us just fine. It had been a long hot summer, and we had spent most of it, seemingly, in the car. So, for Jack to be racing at his local track a ten-minute drive away, was bliss. And if only one of his upcoming mounts could win, that would really be the icing on the cake!

Sixty-two winners in twelve months and well over a million dollars in mount purse earnings for his bug year would have made him champion apprentice most years back in the UK. Jack had come to a new country, unannounced, and built up his business from scratch, meeting new people, riding for new trainers, learning about horse racing in North America, learning about race riding in North America. Learning about life in North America.

Bugs, scratches, crispy horses, rank horses, breezing, lugging in, lugging out. The gate, one turn, two turns, first quarter, half, final quarter, moving his tack, taking his book, picking up mounts, doughnuts to the winning barns in the mornings, slop, mud, off the turf. Highways, interstates, gas stations, apartments, stores, carryout, getting the check, checking account. Hooking up with new friends, going to new restaurants, "sound's good. It's all good!" Movies, meals out, sunbathing on friend's boats on the lake. Lounging in the water, in the sun, on huge inner tubes. Going to the shooting range, looking at guns, looking at Dad, deciding no.

All of these things he saw and experienced and learned.

Should we have come? Should we have given up what we had, the little we had? Would Jack have been better off staying in the UK? Maybe. Maybe not.

But we couldn't know that back then. Back then, he was five feet nine, sixteen years old, getting a ride a week, just starting out. One of many apprentices in town, one of more than a hundred in the country. I had seen how it is for most horsemen there—stable staff, trainers, and jockeys. Most of them work hard every day, yet struggle to pay their bills. Royal Ascot is lovely; the big days are wonderful. But most days aren't big days. Most days are going to Wolverhampton for one. Hours on the road, traffic, and if the horse wins, the rider's and trainer's percentages are next to nothing.

Only a few trainers and jockeys make a good living from horse racing in the UK. Property is expensive; fuel is expensive. With sales tax at twenty percent, everything is expensive. People struggle to get by in the UK. Most people. And there isn't enough sunlight. And the place is so busy, everything is a rush, everything is a queue, everything is a problem.

So, we came to America to see. I wanted to see the country where I was born. Jack wanted to race ride in the USA, and he wanted to earn money. He had seen his parents without a pound in their pocket too often, and he didn't like it. He didn't want to live like that. And I didn't want him to live like that.

And his expectations were higher than mine had been. He is a gifted rider with a strong work ethic. He was born in the sport. Horse racing and Thoroughbreds are the family business, it's in his blood, it's what he has been around since the day he was born.

So, we came, and we saw, and Jack was riding every day there was racing, and he was picking up nice pay-checks. And the cost of living is cheaper here. Property is relatively inexpensive and nice. And after our cold draughty old home in the UK, it was nice to be able to wander around the house in a T-shirt when it was snowing outside. And our bills were a fraction of what they were in the UK, and life went at a more relaxed pace. And the sun shone. And Jack was good.

And Vicky, the mother and wife, well she came out of duty. And I am pleased to say she really enjoys living in America, and that she is now never happier than when driving her little pickup truck on a bright, blue skied day, with country music playing on the radio!

For me, though, for a long time I felt like it had happened too late. That my roots were maybe too deep in the UK. My life had been lived there. I had trained in Newmarket for nearly twenty years. That was who I was. And now that was who I had been. And here I was no one. Just a strange middle-aged man getting in the way.

So, for a long time I missed what I had left behind. Newmarket.

Newmarket Heath. A rugged, sometimes cruel place. But romantic, and impossibly wonderful, with the history of England running through it. Kings and mistresses, and gamblers and drinkers, and jockeys and trainers, and lads and lasses, and aristocrats and millionaires and scoundrels, and wives and lovers. And horses, always horses, beautiful, magnificent, swift, flighty, at the heart of it all. The sport of kings.

The stables, some hundreds of years old. The strings of horses exercising as they have done there for centuries. The

United States of America was still just a foolish dream back then, still an enormous unspoilt wilderness, when racing horses were first training on Newmarket Heath.

By the time the Pilgrims landed at Plymouth in 1620, James I had already built a palace in Newmarket, from where he could pursue his favourite sports.

By the time the American colonists made the Declaration of Independence in 1776, the premises I trained from in Newmarket were already in use as a racing stable.

I miss all of that. All of that history, all of the pageantry, the green turf. The noise, the bustle, the shouting, the swearing, the seeming importance of something that should be so unimportant. The intensity of it all. Over two thousand of the best-bred Thoroughbred racehorses in the world, jostling to use the training gallops. Horses, literally, everywhere.

But now I am in Kentucky. Our home and stables are not ours anymore. Our horses are not with us now. But the heath is still there, and horses still train on it. The world continues to turn, but Newmarket stays the same. It doesn't change. It hasn't really changed in four hundred years. Newmarket is always there. They say you can't go back. But you can, to Newmarket. It is the exception.

For now, though, I am here. Experiencing the great continent of North America, the land of my birth. Born in New York in 1965 to a father from several generations of New Yorkers who hailed originally from Ireland, and a mother with an Irish mother and father, but born in Brixton London.

And now I was here in Lexington, Kentucky, via London, and Newmarket, and England.

Lexington didn't exist when our home in Newmarket was built. When the Georgian pile was being constructed as a gentleman's country house and racing stables, Native Americans were roaming freely across Kentucky.

Kentucke—land of meadows, in the Iroquois language. And I think maybe it is the natural beauty of the state that we have enjoyed the most. We love the weather, the four beautiful seasons, the wildlife, the native birds, the red cardinals, the mature trees in the neighbourhoods. And we like downtown, the restaurants, the bars, the American architecture. The bit of American history there.

Everything seems clean and new here, except, maybe occasionally, when you drive around a corner and find some older part of town, run-down, unused now, old warehouses, waiting for American invention and ideas and can-do to bring it back to life. And it will. Especially here. Lexington is a hipster's dream. A college town, liberal, progressive. Craft beers, craft doughnuts, craft coffee, craft everything. Restaurants spring up everywhere.

Ambitious youngsters are limited only by their imagination here. Start-up costs are low for those with an idea and ambition. And the local population is educated, and the people here are genuinely laid-back and friendly and enthusiastic and positive. American traits.

And all around Lexington are the horses, on the farms, grazing. Pristine farms, paddocks neatly fenced, grass mown.

Everything fresh and painted. Nearby Midway is a delight, a tiny, comatose little town just up the road with a couple of nice restaurants, quaint old Kentucky buildings in gaily painted colours, antiques stores, art galleries - and a railway track running right through the centre of it.

And then of course, Keeneland. The jewel in the crown. The thing, more than anything else, that puts Lexington on the world map. One of the reasons this city in the Midwest feels cosmopolitan, international.

Keeneland sales sell more Thoroughbred bloodstock, for more money, than any other auction house in the world. It is preeminent. If money is important, then Keeneland sales are important.

How important? Well, it is said that Blue Grass airport, across the road from the auction house, extended its runway just to accommodate one of the auction house's leading customer's private jumbo jet.

People come from all over the world to the sales and races at Keeneland. Rich people come. People looking to spend obscene amounts of money come. People accustomed to winning, who now want to win on the racetrack. It is a circus, a bedlam, a brothel, a show.

Horse racing is maybe the truest sporting analogy to life. And life, at the end of the day, comes down to sex. So wealthy people bid against each other for the products of the most expensive studs on earth. And they do that here. At Keeneland, in Lexington. And Jack was part of all this now.

In the thick of it, caught up in it all, a performer in the most colourful show on Earth.

I have cousins all over the States now. They have migrated from New York over the years for their careers. Most of them came to Keeneland that autumn, for the end of Jack's bug year, for my birthday, and really, just as a reason to see each other again. The Gilligans are a close-knit family, and they flew and drove in from Massachusetts, Florida, Michigan, and California. And my sister and brother flew over from England and Ireland. And we were all together again for the first time since we were little kids.

And we watched Jack's eight rides trail home. But no one cared, they shouted for him before the race, celebrated the first Gilligan to be a professional athlete. Made a fuss of him. Had fun, asked him questions. We ate and drank and talked and laughed. And although everyone was older, everything, in a way, was still the same. Everyone was still the same. My Boston cousin was crazy as a teenager, and now he is a sixty-year-old father and lawyer. He got himself banned from a Waffle House during the visit. They can drink, the Gilligans. And they can talk. And they laugh and love too, and care. And they loved Vicky and Jack. And they came to see us in Kentucky, and made us feel at home.

The following week, after they had gone, Jack had more rides booked at Keeneland. These were to be the last of his mounts where he could claim his allowance. The last of his rides as an apprentice. The next week, he would be riding at level weights against the senior jockeys. So a Keeneland winner now would be very timely.

It was the first race on the first day of the racing week. Just a $10,000 claimer, as small as races get there. Only five runners, but the mare was still 23/1.

They broke nicely; it was a mile race around two turns. Two went on, the other three, including Jack, sat off the pace, stalking. They stayed like that along the backstretch until they entered the home turn, when he began to ask the mare for an effort, and, unlike the others he had been riding lately, she responded. She started to pick up, started to close on the two leaders, and as they began to enter the homestretch, she was only two lengths off them, then one, then she picked up the second horse, and we started shouting, and she passed it and moved into second. But then the leader took off; it went away and won easily in the end. And Jack could do nothing about it. They were just second best that day.

And that was as close as he got. That was all she would give him. Keeneland. The beautiful, unrequiting coquette. Playing her old game on him. Spurning his youthful, eager advances still.

Jack rode nearly seven hundred races in his bug year and probably rode nearly another seven hundred breezes. He won sixty-two races and placed in another one hundred and fifty. He rode and placed in stakes races, won at Churchill Downs, won at Kentucky Downs, won at seven different North American tracks, placed at Keeneland. He got years' worth of experience in one. He did years' worth of work in one.

He had only just turned nineteen, and he was now a professional jockey. Something he had told his mother and father he would be since he was a tiny, blond haired, blue-eyed kid running around our stable yard. I like that in a man.

And I am pleased to say, that two years on from his bug year he is riding even more successfully in Kentucky. Riding more winners in better races, his career still on the upward curve, still ascending that mountain, two hundred winners and counting. Stakes success. Keeneland winners! She finally relented…

As for me. Well I'd thought maybe I was coming to America for my career too. But it seems I didn't. It turned out that I came back to look for my father. A small kid in a gold jacket, still stuck somewhere inside me, looking for his dad. He wasn't here, of course. He hadn't been anywhere for a long time.

I remember still, being sat on the couch, tiny, petrified, uncomprehending, as I watched my father's drunken violent anger. And then we were gone. And then he was gone. And people have worse stories than that. But it was not talked about, nothing was ever explained. So, it sat there, in a room in my mind, with the door shut. The same reel playing again and again. So that, even on the best days, there was a problem deep down, still to be dealt with.

But it never was. I didn't admit it had scarred me. Because I didn't even understand it had scarred me.

When I came here though, I started to realize that maybe there was something wrong with me.

I could hide in Newmarket. Just one more crazy trainer among a lot of crazy trainers. But here I had no horses to offer succour, no career to hide behind, no town full of madness to blend into. Here, I was exposed. And for the first time in my life, I realized that all those people who for all those years had said I was crazy, mad…For the first time in my life, I realized they hadn't been joking.

We had only been in the country a couple of months when it happened. We were returning from Indiana Grand where Jack had ridden one in an early race, when we got word that there had been an incident at the track. A horse had clipped heels, stumbled, and lost its rider midway through a race. They said it was bad.

When we got home, I phoned Oriana Rossi, a jockey friend based at Indiana, who years previously had worked for me in Newmarket. She said it was very bad.

Juan Saez and Jack were the only two apprentices on the Kentucky circuit that year getting regular business. It was a spare mount, Juan Saez took it. I drove Jack home. Juan Saez never went home again. He came from a family of top jockeys and was a serious rider winning a lot of races. Everyone knew he would reach the top. *Everyone* knows nothing do they? He was only sixteen years old. Just a kid. Supposed to be just starting out.

Just months later, Oriana was paralyzed in another accident at the same track.

It's a hell of a thing to ride a racehorse. Isn't it?

I went and saw her in the hospital twice. She was unconscious, tubes and wires everywhere. Her mother had flown over from Europe. She was there, sat beside her daughter, helpless. I couldn't go there again.

And that was it, really. I was empty, numb, distraught. The small spark that had still been there was all gone now. I was *The hollow man*. Awake in the tender hours. Surrounded by blackness. Head full of straw. Scared all the time. Anxious all the time. Whatever solace, whatever comfort working with horses had given me all those years—and they did give me something—was gone now. They were gone now. I went through the motions. I carried on. But, over time, slowly, I went empty. There was nothing left, no fight left. I had been fighting too long.

One day, quite a while later, a friend gave me a lady's number. He said I should talk to her; he said she was good. I didn't want to, but eventually, I went. She was a counsellor. And she talked to me. And she asked me questions and gave me some explanations. And it helped a bit, to talk to someone.

And then, one day, she asked me about my father. And I started to tell her about him, and then I began to cry. And I don't know if it surprised her. But it absolutely shocked me. I had no idea. I just thought I didn't think or speak about my father because he hadn't been in my life much. I had no idea, all of those years, that I didn't think about him, because I didn't want to.

And this didn't just happen once; it happened every time I tried to speak to her about him. And I am not the crying type. I don't know if you have ever seen the movie *Analyze This,* but if you have, basically, the Robert De Niro character was me.

So over time, with her help, I began to realize that the spark, the edge I had in me, wasn't so much energy, or ambition, or testosterone. It was pain, and hurt, and fear, and anger. It was about all those emotions I had experienced when I was a small child, that had never been dealt with, never been processed.

Nothing had ever been discussed. Nothing had ever been talked about. No one had ever tried to explain to me what was happening, what was going on. So the grieving process had never happened for me. All of those years, and part of me was still stuck in the past, it lay there still, hidden in the back of my mind, and it influenced who I was, how I processed what life was, what it could be. What it couldn't be for me.

She talked to me about something called abandonment theory. And I was able to understand myself better, to see. And after a while, one day, she asked me to write a letter to my dead father. It was hard. I didn't want to. I didn't know what I would say. But eventually, when I had run out of excuses, one day I did. And it was okay. And I cried again. And I felt something leave me, I felt a release. It really did feel like a weight was lifted from me. And, after all those years, after all that distance, I grieved for my father. And I was finally able to take off that gold jacket, that had gotten so tight I couldn't breathe anymore.

I am not someone who spends his time reading greater meaning into situations. But somehow, I ended up returning to America, a place that was always there, somewhere in my mind, all that time. And in the end, it seems I did have some unfinished business here. I never did find my tractor or Tonka crane though.

I am not all fixed and normal now; I am not completely different than before. But I am a bit better; I feel that I am living more fully in the present. I don't feel, anymore, like my path through life is up a never-ending hill that I must climb wearing a heavy, burdensome coat. And that feels good.

While the cousins were in town we hired a room, and brought in some food, and set up a bar, and put up some balloons and banners. And we celebrated Jack's apprentice year, and my birthday, and being together.

And we hooked up the big TV and replayed some of Jack's winners. And the cousins shouted him home like they had their last fifty on him, and we whooped and cheered and laughed.

And then we put on an old DVD we had from back home, which we had nearly forgotten about. My father, when we were small, had bought a movie camera to film us as kids and to use for family occasions. And, after his death, my mother had taken possession of the films, and we used to watch them sometimes, when we were very young. But over the years, the film footage became corrupted and much of it was lost. Before it was all gone, though, my mother had taken what was left to someone who transferred what they could onto a DVD. We hadn't seen it in years.

So, we sat together, my brother, my sister, my cousins, my wife, and my son. And we put on the film, and we were transported back. My cousins had never seen it. Never knew it existed. Their late parents were there again, laughing and playing up for the silent footage, younger than we were now.

My parents were there, together. My father, slim and young and smart and handsome and smiling. And my mother, young and beautiful. She has Alzheimer's now and just sits silently. But back then, she was vivacious and the life of the party

And we were all there. Little kids. Not knowing what was ahead, not knowing anything. Brought into the world by the adults around us, helped by them, let down by them, shaped by them. As we consciously and unconsciously shape our children now. No horses back then. Just New York in the 1960s, everyone dressed like film stars. Summer and winter, Christmas and christenings, all there, briefly, in grainy, faded, colour footage.

The adults there are all gone now, except my mother. My grandparents were there, even longer gone. Back then they didn't know, didn't think. Back then they were living their lives, passing through this world, probably dreaming of more, settling for less, having mostly decent lives.

They didn't know that someday that footage my father was filming would be all that was left of them. And that the one who would be gone first was the one who did the most to keep the memory of them alive for the longest, the one who cared enough to go out and buy a movie camera, just so he could capture treasured moments with his young family.

Those images are all that is left of them now; our memories of them the only ones there are. But they are not gone completely, because some of what they were is passed on, through their genes and their memes, to Jack and his cousins. Whispers of all those ancestors within them, the next generation, living on into the future. And who knows where life will lead them. Who knows how the tapestry will unfurl. Who knew it would bring us here?

So how was our journey? Was it a success?

Well, Jack Gilligan came to America determined to become a successful thoroughbred jockey in Kentucky, and he realized his dream! He rides successfully, makes good checks, keeps buying cars! And has a great lifestyle.

As for me. Well I came to America determined to become a successful racehorse trainer. And I ended up in therapy…

But you know, on reflection, looking back. I think I got what I needed, if not what I wanted. And actually I feel very grateful for that.

Will Jack Gilligan stay in America? Will we? I don't know. But we are still here now, two years later. Will Newmarket drag us all back, as it does so many, its spell hard to break? It's possible.

It feels like a lot of things are possible now.

Jack Gilligan
Apprentice Year Total: 62 wins

157 placed (2nd & 3rd)

699 rides

$1.23 million purse money won by mounts

With thanks to all who supported Jack with mounts during his bug year, and special thanks to the winners!

Aleutian Queen, Jeremiah O'Dwyer & Black Sheep Racing.
Bauer, Caryn Vechio.
Honey Train, Paul Mcentee & Andrew C. Ritter.
Bluemymind, Larry Lay & Kumud & Rakesh Sikand.
Abby's Promise, Jeremiah O'Dwyer & Debbie Scott.
La Jolla D'Oro, Ernest Retamoza & Running Grey Stables.
Chief Exchanger, Susan Cooney & Quest Realty.
Whoopie Pie, Tom Bergin & Dede Mcgehee.
Artic Sky, Del Loveland.
Locust Trace, Jeffrey Greenhill & Greenhill Racing Stables.
Cara Marie, Kellyn Gorder & Three Chimneys Farm.
Catchifyoucan, Christina Bini & Lone Pond Racing.
Bluemymind, Larry Lay & Kumud & Rakesh Sikand.
Pyro Slew, Jeremiah O'Dwyer & Thomas Nugent.
Will Gracie Shine, Kim Hammond & Foal Run Farm.
Battlefield Angel, Kellyn Gorder & Martha Jane Mullholland.
Cherokee Beads, Kellyn Gorder & TK Stables.

Hehaz Given, Bryan Metz.

Justfollowmylead, John Rankin.

La Jolla D'Oro, Ernest Retamoza & Running Grey Stables.

Reason To Medal, Bernard Girdley & T. Hasting and C, Keith.

Will Gracie Shine, Kim Hammond & Foal Run Farm.

Eu Bandelero, Edwardo Caramori & Equinox inc.

Underground Valley, Gary Aimonetti & James Arbuckle.

Owl Creek, Kim Hammond & Paul Martin.

Elmor, Jimmy Corrigan & Corrigan Racing Stables.

Bell By The Ridge, Kim Hammond & Merrit Hudson.

Borealis Way, Monica Goetz & John Wentworth.

Will Gracie Shine, Kim Hammond & Foal Run Farm.

Elmor, Jimmy Corrigan & Corrigan Racing Stables.

Indiana Rockey, Kim Hammond & Willowbrook Stables.

Didhementionmyname, Kellyn Gorder & Team Valor.

Memos Lolitas, Rangel Guillermo.

Darwins Dream, John Dyer & Darwin Krentz.

Red Hot Plot, Vernon Coyle.

Followthemoneytrail, Kim Hammond & Willowbrook Stables.

Grand Slam Larry, Larry Lay & Joy Lay.

Reason To Medal, Bernard Girdley & Timothy Hastings.

Feets Afire, Del Loveland.

La Jolla D'Oro, Ernest Retamoza & Running Grey Stables.

Taylor Lane, Michael A. Ewing & Thomas Girardi.

Painted Valley, John Wells & Romar LLC.

Championofjustice, Michael A. Ewing & Thomas Girardi.

Gift Receipt, Michael A. Ewing & Bantry Farms.

Bon Vivant, Paul Mcentee & Andrew Ritter.

Abbys Promise, Jeremiah O'Dwyer & Debbie Scott.

Eufala, Joe Sharp & Dede Mcgehee.

Abbys Promise, Jeremiah & Debbie Scott.

Royal Hush, Tanya Boulmetis & John Harvey.

Honey C, J. Wayne Tapp & Jane Coomes.

Vision Of Liz, Peter Pizzo & Russel Dennis.

Charnocks, Ron Moquett & Southern Springs and S. Sparks.

Shes Messi, Larry Lay & Rakesh and Kumud Sikand.

Shes Lying Again, Don Mills.

Barnyard Fiddler, Don Mills.

Beside Still Water, Victoria Oliver & St George Farm Racing.

Sounds Devine, Sal Guerrero.

Passionforwinning, Faustino Hernandez.

Ubiquitous Mantle, Michael A. Ewing & Northern Lights
    Racing.

Honey C, J. Wayne Tapp &Jane Coomes.

Strumming, Jordan Blair & Kenneth Ayres.

Magna May, Phillip Clark & Norma Clark.

In Memory of Juan Saez.

CPSIA information can be obtained
at www.ICGtesting.com
Printed in the USA
LVHW082114210319
611436LV00014B/43/P